A Textbook of

General Studies

Class XI

By

Aditi Misra

Layout and Design

Aashish Aggarwal

PITAMBAR
PUBLISHING COMPANY
100 Years of Excellence

Published by :
Pitambar Publishing Company Pvt. Ltd.
888, East Park Road, Karol Bagh, New Delhi -110 005
Phones : 011-23673608
E-mail : pitambarpublishing@rediffmail.com
website : www.pitambarising.in

Edition : 2026

ISBN : 978-81-209-1589-3

Price ₹230/-

Printed at : Sachin Print Process Delhi

Preface

The Central Board of Secondary Education (CBSE) had introduced General Studies at the Senior School stage as a part of the implementation of the National Policy on Education, 1986. The earlier guidelines and syllabus, published in 1990, were a concrete step towards providing a value oriented curriculum. It was visualized as a subject that would transcend all disciplines and would bring a positive change in students. To facilitate the students, we had earlier published 'A Textbook of General Studies' for classes XI and XII.

In light of the changing dynamics of today's society, the books for General Studies published by us have been reviewed and revised. The revised books include objectives specific to each unit along with suggested transactional strategies. An attempt has been made to make the content more relevant and interesting for students. These books provide a structure for effective transaction of this subject and at the same time offer ample flexibility to teachers. The teachers may choose readings and transactional approach for each unit as per the interest of students and availability of time.

I wish to thank Ms Leeza Dutta, Kalpana Pant, Mamta Kanti Kumar, Jyotika Kapoor, Kanu Chopra and Rohini Kapoor for their valuable contribution.

It is hoped that the new edition will contribute in development of responsible citizenship among students. I would welcome feedback and suggestions of the readers for further improvement.

– Author

Contents

Syllabus

INTRODUCTION

All students in the academic stream at the Senior School stage are required to study the following eight subjects:

A. Language(s) -Two

Elective I

Elective II

Elective III

(Elective IV is allowed in lieu of a language)

B. Work Experience

Physical and Health Education

General Studies

While subjects under 'A' are evaluated externally, those under 'B' are evaluated internally by the schools. As per the Scheme of Studies, a candidate will be eligible to get the pass certificate of the Board, if he/she gets a grade higher than 'E' in all subjects of internal assessment unless he/she is exempted (Private/Patrachar Vidyalaya and candidates sponsored by Adult School shall be exempted from Work Experience, General Studies and Physical and Health Education). General Studies, one of the three subjects assessed internally by the school, is a very significant component of the overall curriculum as it equips students with the ability to grow into an integrated personality.

The subject of General Studies had been included in the scheme of studies w.e.f. 1989 (1988 for KVS) in pursuance of the National Policy on Education 1986. It is an extension of the following 10 value-oriented curricular components as enumerated in the document 'Programme of Action' which are integrated with the Secondary curriculum:

1. India's Freedom Movement
2. Constitutional Obligations
3. National Identity
4. Cultural Heritage
5. Egalitarianism, Democracy and Secularism
6. Equality of Sexes
7. Protection of Environment
8. Removal of Social Barriers
9. Observance of Small Family Norms
10. Inculcation of Scientific Temper

Aims and Objectives

The purpose of orienting students to General Studies is to develop in them an appreciation for the holistic nature of knowledge. In contemporary times, familiarity with General Studies is indispensable because at the senior school stage there is an element of specialization due to which the students do not get exposed to some vital disciplines/areas of study that are not covered in their specialized field. The whole course of General Studies is, therefore, focused on proper development of the 'affective domain' by exposing the students to varied domains of study.

Specific Objectives

Students will be able to:

1. imbibe scientific temper by developing a rational attitude involving disbelief in superstitions and respect for integrity, objectivity and scientific method;
2. gain awareness about the changing concept of time and space in which mutual interdependence among countries has assumed added significance for the survival of humanity and to accentuate the importance of peace and economic cooperation;
3. highlight the importance of and need for conserving and promoting ecological balance and take practical steps for not only checking the unhindered depletion of natural resources, but also find other alternatives to preserve and enhance them;
4. develop pride in the rich cultural heritage as well as in the multipronged achievements of the country in various fields such as politics, agriculture, Science and technology, education and industry;
5. inculcate constitutional values and imbibe the spirit of secularism and national unity;
6. be conversant with contemporary socio-economic problems of the country like illiteracy, poverty, social disharmony, sex or caste discrimination etc.

The course for General Studies for Classes XI and XII has been revised keeping in mind the changing dynamics of today's society. The purpose behind revising the curriculum is to make it more relevant. It is hoped that this course will develop responsible citizens.

In the following sections, a brief introduction to each unit has been provided, along with its specific objectives. Further, contemporary issues have been included in each unit to make it pertinent to the lives of students. Suggestive transactional strategies have also been incorporated in each unit to facilitate teachers in effectively planning the learning activities. It may be ensured that all learners get the opportunity to express their views during the conduct of the activities.

GUIDELINES TO TEACHERS

It is suggested that the assessment of General Studies be continuous and not a one-time exercise. Further, a variety of assessment tools may be adopted as per the transactional strategies used by the teachers. Rubrics may be developed for evaluating students' work to ensure a fair evaluation. The teacher may also encourage students to engage in self-assessment. The aim of assessing this component is not to evaluate how many facts students may recall, but to ensure that they are sensitized towards the feelings, opinions and viewpoints of others so that they become more tolerant, objective and empathetic. The objective of assessment is to ensure that the students have imbibed the values inherent in the ten value-oriented curriculum components as enumerated in the document 'Programme of Action'. Thus, assessment needs to be continuous and must take into account individual differences in learning. It is advised that schools maintain cumulative records of students' periodic achievements and progress during the year as these are subject to the scrutiny of the Board as and when deemed fit.

The teacher may adopt any one or more transactional strategies from those listed in this document. This list is not exhaustive. Further, only examples of some topics of the unit are given. Similar exercises for other topics may be developed.

An example of a rubric for role play organized by students to present the life history of freedom fighters, is given below:

Objectives: After the role play, students will be able to:

1. outline the challenges that freedom fighters faced
2. appreciate the contribution of freedom fighters
3. delineate the significant life events of Indian freedom fighters
4. respect our nation's freedom
5. appreciate the democratic ethos of our country.

The teacher may give the following instructions to the students:

- You may work in groups of five/six.
- Each group will select an Indian freedom fighter and gather information on his/her life history.
- Each group will present the life history of the selected freedom fighter in the form of a role play.
- After the presentation, other groups will share their views on the role play presented.

The rubric for assessment of this activity is given below.

Areas	1	2	3
Factual Information on the Topic	Inaccurate information. Lacks relevant information	Factual information is mostly accurate. Adequate information	Factual information is accurate. In-depth information
Attitude	The student is not open to ideas of others during planning and discussion.	The student accepts most ideas without negative comments.	The student is open to ideas of others during planning and discussion.
Participation in Group Work	Uninterested	Limited participation	Active participation
Presentation	Incoherent, not interesting for audience	Engages audience intermittently	Innovative, engaging and entertaining.

In this example, a maximum of 12 marks may be awarded as each of the four dimensions may be scored on a scale of 1-3. Similarly, rubrics for assessment of other activities may be developed taking help from the assessment criteria given in the Formative Assessment Manuals, Classes IX & X, developed by the CBSE.

The evaluation of General Studies is done by the schools. They are expected to assess the performance of all the students on a 9-Point scale as given below and report it to the Board:

A-l : Topi/8th of the passed candidates

A-2 : Next 1/8* of the passed candidates

B-l : Next 1/8* of the passed candidates

B-2 : Next 1/8* of the passed candidates

C-l : Next 1/8* of the passed candidates

C-2 : Next 1/8* of the passed candidates

D-l : Next 1/8* of the passed candidates

D-2 : Next 1/8* of the passed candidates

E : Failed candidates

Since the above definitions are based on large statistics of the Board, they will not be applicable to a school situation. What is expected from the schools is to make an assessment keeping general performance of students who take the Board's Examinations in mind and to award grades in such a way that the student should get the grade according to the group he is likely to belong if he is considered to be a part of the total population.

Passing in General Studies is a basic condition of eligibility for earning the Senior School Certificate from the Board. The result of a student who fails to get a grade higher than 'E' in General Studies will be withheld but not for more than a year. This arrangement imposes an additional responsibility on the teaching staff of a school.

As has been emphasized, the major objectives of teaching General Studies lie in the 'affective domain'. Accordingly, evaluation should be based on observational methods assessing students' interests, attitudes and personality traits.

GENERAL STUDIES: CLASS XI

UNIT I: SCIENCE AND TECHNOLOGY

Humankind has constantly sought to innovate to make life more comfortable. Almost every aspect of our life today is touched by Science in one way or the other. It is pertinent that we are able to identify and appreciate the varied applications of Science in our daily lives. Whether it was learning to domesticate animals rather than hunt, or inventing the wheel, we have sought to better our lives through scientific inventions and discoveries. These changes have impacted modern technology the most. Rapid changes in the field of Science have led to tremendous advances in the field of technology and that has had both positive and negative impacts on the society at large. For example, culture of organs could be life saving in case of emergency but also has given rise to heated debates on ethics and abuse vs. application. This unit throws light upon the integral relation between Science and Technology.

The objectives of this unit are to:

- highlight Science as a necessary part of our everyday life.
- explore emerging technologies.
- analyze the impact of Science and emerging technologies on our lives. Content

I Application of Science in everyday life

- Identifying role of Science in daily activities e.g. cooking, communication, transportation etc.
- Improving life through knowledge of Science

II Emerging technologies

- Green technology
- Mechatronics
- Nanotechnology
- Biotechnology

III Science and Technology in the social context

- Science: discussion on use & abuse
- Uses and misuses of technology (in healthcare, agriculture, warfare, changing lifestyle etc.)
- Assistive technology for the differently abled

Suggested Transactional Strategies:

Students may:

1. prepare a projects (in groups of 5-7 students) where some models based on emerging technologies may be presented and explained such as solar panels, rain water harvesting, e-waste management, etc.
2. organize a cyber safety day in the school. This may be suitably done during the morning assembly or activity period.
3. debate on the pros and cons of using social media, or on any other related topic.
4. enumerate ways in which Science and technology have changed lives particularly in the context of differently abled children.

UNIT II: UNDERSTANDING SOCIAL STRUCTURE

Social structure is the distinctive, stable arrangement of institutions, whereby, human beings in a society interact and live together. These arrangements may take the form of kinship, marriage, language, caste, politics, economy and so on. Various social institutions function in tandem with each other to fabricate a social structure which affects individuals and in turn individuals impact social structures. This unit helps in understanding the social structure of society, its dynamics and the various forces that shape it.

The objectives of this unit are to:

- acquaint the students with the basic and distinctive features of the society they live in.
- enable the students to understand different types of social institutions of their society.
- understand the functions and significance of different social institutions of Indian society.

Content

I. Meaning and importance of society and social structure/s.

II. Distinctive features of Indian society

III. Social institutions of Indian society

- Family and marriage
- Religion
- Economy
- Politics

IV. Unity in diversity

V Continuity and change in Indian society

Suggested Transactional Strategies:

Students may:

1. conduct a survey in the school, exploring the relationship between economic status and occupation.
2. document examples of social relations witnessed by them in their neighbourhood. They may then work in groups and prepare a small skit showcasing the same.
3. prepare a questionnaire containing 5-7 questions, collect data and analyze the findings by seeking opinion from different people of various age groups on different social institutions.
4. work in groups of 5-6 and present a glimpse of Indian culture by preparing scrapbooks, collecting photographs or making powerpoint presentations.

UNIT III: PROTECTION OF ENVIRONMENT

The Earth Charter says, "humanity is a part of the vast evolving universe. Earth, our home, is alive with a unique community of life. The forces of nature make existence a demanding and uncertain adventure but Earth has provided the conditions essential to life's evolution. The protection of Earth's vitality, diversity and beauty is a sacred trust."

The many shlokas and hymns of the Vedas have shaped Indian philosophy in terms of being frugal with the Earth's resources so that there is enough for all. These ideas and thoughts have been replicated in many sustainable development goals and Earth environment summits in the past few years. Thus, this unit proposes to describe the connection between availability and usage of resources.

The objectives of this unit are to:

- identify the available natural resources.
- create awareness about factors causing the depletion of natural resources.
- discuss the implications of the rising world population.
- outline the importance of and need for conserving and promoting ecological balance.
- inspire students to adopt an environment friendly lifestyle. Content

I. Natural resources
  - Renewable
  - Non renewable

II. Factors causing environmental pollution and degradation

III. Understanding sustainable development

IV. Strategies for environmental conservation

V. Lifestyle changes for environmental protection

- generating less waste
- environment friendly transportation
- Recycle - Reduce - Reuse - Refuse - Renew - Recover

Suggested Transactional Strategies:

Students may:

1. make presentations on initiatives and conservation movements made by individuals and organizations.
2. study their surroundings, enlist local species and learn more about them.
3. design a plan to keep the school premises clean and save paper/paper/ electricity.
4. attempt an audit of water/electricity use at home/ in the school and explore the possibility for reducing their consumption.

UNIT IV: NATIONAL UNITY

A nation is a unified socio-economic and political structure. It denotes a body of people who have a feeling of oneness, built on the basis of common history, society, culture and values. This feeling of oneness binds the people together in to a nation. National integration is the awareness of a common identity amongst the citizens of a country. It means that though the individuals belong to different communities, castes, religions, cultures and regions and speak different languages, all of them recognize the fact that they are one. This kind of integration is very important in the building of a strong and prosperous nation. This unit provides a comprehensive insight into India's national integration.

The objectives of this unit are to:

- discuss the meaning and importance of national integration.
- appreciate how the national movement against British rule helped in national integration.
- identify the challenges to national integration in our country.
- appreciate the concept of secularism in the Indian context. Content

I. Understanding the meaning and importance of national integration

- Unified socio-economic, political structure and feeling of oneness on the basis of common history, society, values and culture
- Integration - fusion of norms and cultures- sharing of values

II. Role of national movement in national integration

- Freedom struggle
  - ▣ Non-cooperation movement

- ▣ Civil disobedience movement
- ▣ Quit India movement

• Role of Mahatma Gandhi in mass mobilization- awakening of national feeling among masses

IV. Challenges to national integration

• Forces causing a divide among the people of the nation

- ▣ Casteism
- ▣ Communalism

V. Promoting national integration

• National symbols and their significance

• Heroic deeds and sacrifices of freedom fighters

• History of the country and its cultural diversity

• Importance of unity in the country in the midst of diversity

• Importance of Republic Day and Independence Day

VI. Secularism

• Constitutional provisions

• Freedom of conscience, thought and expression

Suggested Transactional Strategies:

Students may:

1. form a Youth Parliament in the class. It may function through a democratic process of working by choosing a cabinet, discussion and voting on a bill relating to prescribed dress code for students in educational institutions.
2. collect passages/quotes with universal messages from world literature and these may be posted on display boards.
3. write creative slogans on the themes that unite people of different communities, for example, music, cricket, etc, and present them on display boards.
4. read selected biographies of great leaders and organize book discussions.
5. actively participate in NCC, NSS, Scouting and Guiding activities.

UNIT V: INTERNATIONAL UNDERSTANDING

The significance of international understanding and cooperation are of paramount importance. Rapid advances in technology have remarkably connected the world and the boundaries between global and local seem to be fading away. In such a scenario, maintaining peace and harmony among nations is of paramount significance. International organizations, like the United Nations, provide a platform to different nations to negotiate and reach common ground on various unsettled issues. Today, awareness about various concerns related to international understanding is necessary to become a responsible global citizen. Therefore, this unit focuses on various dimensions of international understanding.

The objectives of this unit are to:

- acquaint the students with the need, scope and importance of international understanding.
- elaborate the structure, types and functions of different international organizations working for international harmony.
- outline the importance of human rights with special reference to women and children.
- create awareness about the importance of their rights and duties towards clean environment, peace and mutual cooperation.
- throw light upon how interdependence among countries has assumed added significance for the survival of humanity.
- outline the importance of peace and economic cooperation.

Content

I. Meaning of internationalism and international understanding. Perspective on global citizenship

II. Need, scope, dimensions and basic principles of international understanding

III. International organizations and forums working for mutual cooperation and international understanding

IV. Place and role of human rights in international understanding

V. Peace conventions, international cooperation on environment and climate change

Suggested Transactional Strategies:

The students may:

1. read selected material, for example, "Education for International Understanding" by Reuben R. Palm, United Nations brochure on peace keeping .
2. work in pairs and visit the websites of different international organizations, for example, UNICEF or UNESCO. They may then act as representatives of these organizations and a mock press conference may be arranged, where some students may ask questions about the ongoing projects, policies and mandates of the chosen organizations.
3. discuss how advances in technology have changed the dynamics of international understanding. The students' inputs may be recorded by a

representative chosen by the class. The class may be asked to submit an article for the school magazine based on the discussion.

4. conduct a model UN peace convention wherein they will represent different countries to discuss how they can work together to promote universal harmony, for example, through the conduct of sports/cultural/literature festivals, etc.
5. prepare a presentation for the class on issues concerning women, children, elderly and persons with special needs in contemporary times.
6. enlist their rights and the corresponding responsibility for each. This may be followed by a discussion on what measures may be taken if one's rights are violated.

1 Science, Technology and Society

INTRODUCTION

We live in the age of science. The evolution of science and technology has dramatically changed the course of world history. People all over the world, use and benefit from modern technology, and the tremendous opportunities it provides. It plays a significant role in almost all fields of human life. Technology has simplified the access to many necessary tools people need in various spheres of life including education, industry, medicine, communication and transportation. However, excessive usage of technology has its drawbacks. Although, in most cases, the speed of fulfilling tasks accelerates with the help of technology, many people do not realize that technology has also negatively affected society, and its considerable development has complicated life in a number of different ways.

Science and technology are related to each other. The word science originates from the Latin word 'scientia' which means knowledge. It formulates theories and laws. Technology, originates from the Greek word 'technologia' which means the study of art and skill. Technology is an applied science.

IMPACT OF SCIENCE ON SOCIETY

Although modern science is of relatively recent origin, having started with Galileo about 350 years ago, it has made rapid progress and completely transformed the manner of our living. It is said that our life has changed more in the last one hundred years than it did in thousands of years because of the scientific knowledge accumulated over the last three centuries, and its application in the form of technology.

ACTIVITY

List any two items used by your family in daily life, classified on the basis of the stated time period of invention given below in the table.

Aim: Comprehending the progress of science and technology.

Procedure: The students can fill the chart below based on their findings.

Name of the gadget/ instrument	1970-95	1995-2010	2010 onwards
Mobile phone			

About 200 years ago the pace of technology in society began to quicken. Wind, water and animal power with the limitation of their place and capacity were supplemented and then replaced by the steam engine, which went on to power the factories for the industrial revolution. The rail road made it possible to move things and people over great distances quickly. The telegraph and later the telephone carried communication. Electric lighting replaced the dim glow of the kerosene and gas.

By the beginning of the twentieth century, the notion of progress was closely linked with technological development. The automobile and air plane not only changed travel but also the nature of our cities and towns. Radio and then television brought more of the outside world into everyone's homes. Knowledge about the cause of diseases brought new treatment and preventive measures. Computers were invented and today the internet is used by a vast majority and has been an integral part of the electronic revolution. Today, all electronic devices are manufactured keeping the internet and connectivity in mind. Technologies such as General Packet Radio Service (GPRS), Global Positioning System (GPS) are built on internet and satellite technology and have made the world a global village.

Will cloud computing revolutionize the IT industry?

Many people are already using cloud computing without realizing it. Examples include communication tools such as Skype, web-based e-mail like Gmail and Hotmail, video sites like YouTube, I-Cloud. Cloud computing enables users to store files and software remotely, rather than on a hard drive or server at their office.

The accumulation of scientific knowledge and new technologies has transformed human lives. It has helped provide many with cleanliness, nutrition, medical care, transport and entertainment not available and known two centuries ago. These varied technologies have also presented us with a difficult question about how to use science most effectively to meet human needs.

APPLICATION OF SCIENCE IN EVERYDAY LIFE

Science affects us all, every day of the year, from the moment you wake up, all day long, and through the night. The alarm clock, the weather report, the road you drive on, the bus you ride in, your decision to order and eat pizza, instead of meal at home, your cell phone, the antibiotics that treat your sore throat, the clean water that comes from your tap, and the light that you turn off at the end of the day, have all been brought to you by science. The modern world would not be modern at all without the understandings and technology enabled by science.

We live in a world that is constantly growing smaller and smaller with each new technological development and scientific advancement. Society has been speeding up and we have shifted from a world of 'I want this soon' to a world of 'I want this now'. This new way of thinking is possible only with the technological advancements of our time.

Multimedia presentations and internet used as teaching tools

1. Education is developing and fast changing. In fact, innovations in education are a must to keep pace with the changing world. The use of technology is one of these innovations. Today projectors, multimedia presentations and internet are used as teaching tools. The learning capabilities of people vary from audio to visual. Visual presentation through technological devices facilitates easy understanding. Instant access to virtual class rooms, e-library broadens the horizon of teacher and the taught.

2. The food we eat is a result of various scientific practices which have resulted in providing food in large quantities for the growing population across the globe. Science has transformed

the way we eat today. In the 1940's, biologists began developing high-yielding varieties of corn, wheat, and rice, which, when paired with new fertilizers and pesticides developed by chemists, dramatically increased the amount of food that could be harvested from a single field, ushering in the Green Revolution. These science-based technologies triggered striking changes in agriculture, massively increasing the amount of food available to feed the world and simultaneously, transforming the economic structure of agricultural practices. Without science, it would not have been possible to match the food requirement for the growing population.

Food from across the globe

Science gives us safe food, free from harmful bacteria, in clean containers or hygienic tins. It also teaches us to eat properly, indicating a diet balanced in protein, carbohydrate and containing vitamins. The results are freedom from disease and a prolonged quality life. In pre-scientific days, food was monotonous and sometimes dangerous; today it is safe and varied. It is varied because of improved sea. land and air transport: food can now be freely imported and exported.

3. Today with medicines, varied scientific tools and application, we can live a better quality of life. The impact of modern medicine has led to the eradication of smallpox, prevention of nutritional deficiencies and successful treatment of fatal

infections. Scientists are also trying to discover different kinds of medicines and supplements that can help our body fight diseases and cure lifestyle problems.

4. With the introduction of telecommunication and electronic mail, the lives of people became easier and communication among people became convenient. With the advent of modern communication systems like mobiles (smart phones) and internet, people are able to collaborate more effectively. The widespread usage of internet for social networking, example Facebook or Instagram has made communication fast and cost effective. Video-conferencing through Skype has improved communication further. Online messaging platforms like What'sApp have given people the luxury to make their own discussion based chat rooms. There are more ways to socialize now than there used to be in past.

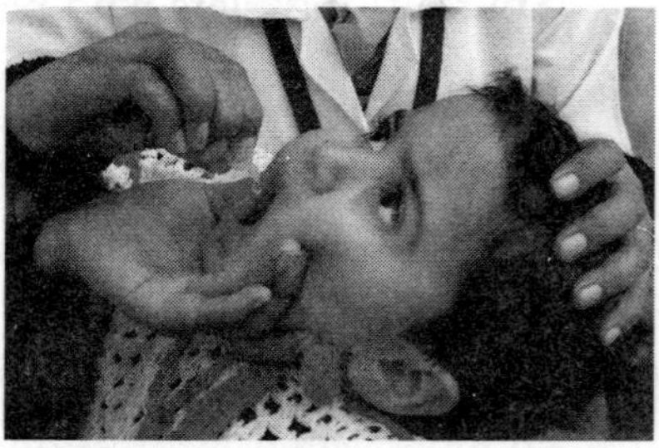

Preventive medicine ensures a healthy life

5. The advent of technology and the use of the internet have affected the way we travel. These changes include our choice of prospective destinations, how we get there, where we stay, and what we do. Digitalization has given us choices

Technology has made the world global village

in mode of travel, data to gather information about the place to be visited and the amount of expense we want to incur. In the digital age, we've become a generation of DIY (Do It Yourself) travellers who plan, manage and make customized travel bookings online.

6. Across the globe, people work on virtual teams, be it by email, online collaboration, messaging, video conferences, or a combination of any of the above. For most of the last century, communicating professionally meant writing letters, sending faxes, or talking on the phone. Email now is the primary means of communication in the modern workplace. We are communicating more and faster. There has been a quantum leap due to the incorporation of technology into the workplace. The major influences are email, business software and smart phones.

ACTIVITY

Decode your thoughts

Aim : Comprehension and analysis of the study material

Procedure : The students will be shown pictures of gadgets used in daily life. They will write advantages and disadvantages of the same.

Home, office and school, all bear witness to the progress and application of science. Nowadays, most homes possess electric lighting and cooking, but many also have washing machines, vacuum cleaners and kitchen appliances, all designed to increase comfort and cleanliness and reduce drudgery. Technology helped by science, produces the fan which cools the air, the machinery which makes the furniture and fabrics and variety of machines which make our life good and easy. The books and papers at school, and again everything from the piece of chalk to the closed-circuit television for instruction are the direct or indirect results of scientific progress.

EMERGING TECHNOLOGIES

Emerging technologies are perceived as novel and relatively fast growing technology, with the potential to exert a considerable impact on the socio-economic structure of the society. Emerging technologies include educational technology, nanotechnology, biotechnology, robotics, artificial intelligence and many more. The choice of a particular technology depends up on its relevance to the country's requirement i.e. the socio-economic conditions of the people. The countries requirement to develop a technology or acquire it depends upon its natural, financial and human resources.

Space Technology

Space technology includes spacecraft, satellites, space stations, support infrastructure, equipment, and procedures. Many common everyday services such as weather forecasting, remote sensing, GPS systems, satellite television, and some long distance communications systems critically rely on space infrastructure. Of the sciences, astronomy and earth science (remote sensing) benefit from space technology. New technologies originating with or accelerated by space-related endeavours are often, subsequently, exploited in varied economic activities.

Space Technology and India

Today, India has acquired eminence in world class space science. It has mastered modern space technology and its various applications for the benefit of society. New space technology is being utilized for telecommunications, television broadcasts, weather watch and for providing information relating to agriculture, forests, water resources and minerals to mention a few.

The Indian Space Research Organisation ISRO was formed first satellite, Aryabhata, which was launched by the Soviet Union in 1975. In 1980 Rohini became the first satellite to be placed in orbit by an Indian made launch vehicle, SLV-3. ISRO, subsequently, developed two other rockets: the Polar Satellite Launch Vehicle (PSLV) for launching satellites into polar orbits and the Geosynchronous Satellite Launch Vehicle (GSLV) for placing satellites into geostationary orbits. These rockets have launched numerous communications satellites and earth observation satellites. ISRO sent one lunar orbiter, Chandrayaan-1, on 22nd October 2008 and Mars orbiter, which successfully entered Mars orbit on 24th September 2014, making India the first nation to succeed on its first attempt, and ISRO the fourth space agency in the world and the first space agency in Asia, to successfully reach the Mars orbit.

Mars Climate Orbiter-2

Dr. Vikram Sarabhai founded India's space program. He founded the Physical Research Laboratory, the Space Science Research Institute, the Department of Space, and the Indian Space Research Organisation (ISRO).

Dr. A. P. J. Abdul Kalam was President of India from 2002 to 2007. He spent four decades as a scientist and science administrator, mainly at the Defence Research and Development Organisation (DRDO) and Indian Space Research Organisation (ISRO). He was intimately involved in India's civilian space program and military missile development efforts.

Functions of the Indian Spacecrafts

1. **Communication Satellites:** Supports and helps in television broadcasting, satellite news gathering, telecommunication, disaster warning ,weather forecasting, search and rescue operation services.

2. **Earth Observation Satellites:** They are the biggest civilian remote sensing satellite constellation in the world, supporting whole host of applications in the areas of cartography. ocean and atmosphere, land and water resources.

3. **Scientific Spacecraft:** Spacecraft for research in areas like planetary and earth sciences, atmospheric sciences, astronomy, theoretical physics and astrophysics.

4. **Navigation Satellites:** Satellites for navigation services to meet the emerging demands of the civil aviation requirements.

5. **Experimental Satellites:** A host of small satellites meant for experimental purposes. These experiments include remote sensing and atmospheric studies.

6. **Small Satellites:** Sub 500 kg class satellites - a platform for stand-alone payloads for earth imaging and science missions within a quick turnaround time.
7. **Student Satellites:** ISRO's Student Satellite programme, envisaged to encourage various universities and institutions for the development of Nano/Pico Satellites.

Indian space scientists foresee several developments in the new millennium when they can scale new heights. Revolutionary developments in the fields of communication, information and micro- electronics are driving greater convergence and forging new directions for aerospace programmes. On February 15, 2017, India launched 104 satellites in a single flight from Sriharikota.

Electronics

Electronics is a branch of science that deals with the study of flow and control of electrons (electricity). Electronic components play a key role in our daily life. Almost everything that surrounds us has direct link to electronics, from the computers we use to laptops, net books or notebooks which has millions of tiny electronic components on it like resistors, inductors, capacitors, logic gates, to the calculators, appliances, measuring devices, and gadgets to name just a few. Electronics moulds the life we have today. It is the barometer of achievement, if we use the advancement in technology as a yardstick of progress.

Electronic Panel

Important Contributions of Electronics to Humanity

Communications Systems: Today's communication system traces its beginning in the year 1876, when the telephone was invented by Alexander Graham Bell and in the year 1908 when Lee De Forest invented the Triode Vacuum that opened the way for wireless communications. Telephones, mobile phones, internet connectivity, television, radio broadcasting, and other forms of communications would not exists without electronics and its principles behind all of these necessities.

Computers: Computer had its beginning with the invention in 19th century by Professor Charles Babbage. He designed the analytical engine upon which the basic computers today are based. Today, the world has progressed to fifth generation computing devices based on artificial intelligence, application such as voice recognition. The use of parallel processing and superconductors is helping to make artificial intelligence a reality. Quantum computation, molecular and nanotechnology will radically change the face of computers in years to come. The goal of fifth-generation computing is to develop devices that respond to natural language input and are capable of learning and self-organization.

INDIA TO HAVE 70 SUPER COMPUTERS FOR HIGH-LEVEL RESEARCH

The super computer will help India do research in different fields ranging from climate, defence and other areas, which a normal computer is ill-equipped for.

PTI New Delhi, May 24, 2015

The government has begun the process of having 70 super computers in the country, which will enable high-level research in different fields for not only government agencies but also the private sector.

The super computer will help India do research in different fields ranging from climate, defence and other areas, which a normal computer is ill-equipped for. The computer will have a capacity (speed) of half petaflop to 20 petaflop, but by the time the project reaches its full peak, the speed of the super computers can go up to 50 petaflop. A petaflop is a measure of a computer's processing speed and can be expressed as a thousand trillion floating point operations per second. "The project, which costs around Rs 4,500 crore is in its nascent stage. It will come up with association of the Department of Science and Technology (DST) and the Department of Information and Technology (DIT).

Telecommunications Technology

Satellite ground station

Telecommunication is defined as the science and technology of communication over a distance. The ability to convey information quickly, accurately, and efficiently has always been one of the main focuses driving human innovation. From prehistoric man with their signal fires to the smart phone-wielding high-powered executives of today, communication still remains a key for survival and success. The history of telecommunication illustrates this never-ending push for progress as it steadily parallels human growth, becoming more widespread and efficient as the development of modern civilization unfolds.

Remarkable progress in telecommunication technology has had, and will continue to have, an enormous impact on telecommunication manufacturing and service industries. In particular digital technology integrates transmission, switching, processing and retrieval of information, provides opportunities to merge various service modes into integrated whole. Satellite and optical fibre, among other technologies contribute significantly to the globalization of telecommunication. Now with the rapid growth of internet, telecommunications has expanded to include data networks. The newest technologies in telecommunications are wireless devices and wireless data plans. Telecommunications and information-related industries continue to enjoy a rapid growth in the internet and the wireless device and network sectors.

India is currently the world's second-largest telecommunications market and has registered strong growth in the past decade and half. The Indian mobile economy is growing rapidly and will contribute substantially to India's gross domestic product (GDP), according to report prepared by GSM Association (GSMA-Groupe Special Mobile Association) in collaboration with the Boston Consulting Group (BCG).

The liberal and reformist policies of the Government of India have been instrumental along with strong consumer demand in the rapid growth in the Indian telecom sector. The government has enabled easy market access to telecom equipment and a fair and proactive regulatory framework that has ensured availability of telecom services to consumer at affordable prices. The deregulation of foreign direct investment (FDI) norms has made the sector one of the fastest growing and a top five employment opportunity generator in the country. The GSMA represents the interests of mobile operators worldwide, uniting nearly 800 operators with more than 250 companies in the broader mobile ecosystem.

Nuclear Energy

As the world population continues to grow and development increases so does the demand for energy. Fossil fuels are burned and used in generation of energy because the technology exists and at the moment, they are widely available. However, as countries develop further, their sources of energy will also change. They will probably still be heavily dependent on fossil fuels, but will begin to use more renewable energy. The reason for the change are; greater concern for the environment; rising prices and finite nature of fossil fuels. Nuclear energy aims to reduce the reliance on fossil fuel for importing countries.

Nuclear power plant

Nuclear power has created widespread debate, because some people see it as a solution to declining fossil fuels while others worry about the waste produced, the technology falling into the wrong hands and accidents. The world's two biggest nuclear accidents in recent times are: Chernobyl (Ukraine) in 1986 and Fukushima (Japan) in 2011. The Fukushima accident was caused by a giant earthquake and tsunami that hit the east coast of Japan on 11th March 2011.

The advantages of nuclear energy are many: there is an abundant supply of uranium; the raw material for nuclear energy releases very low amounts of greenhouse gases; it reduces the dependency on oil, coal and gas; nuclear waste can be safely stored underground.

The disadvantages of nuclear energy are; the risk of nuclear accidents; the nuclear power stations can become terrorist targets; use of nuclear technology to make nuclear weapons; transporting nuclear material and nuclear waste is hazardous and expensive; nuclear power stations only have a limited life period and the cost of decommissioning them is expensive; living next to nuclear power stations can increase the risk of cancer. People don't want nuclear power stations built near where they live. Mining for uranium is dangerous and can be polluting. Nuclear waste remains radioactive for thousands of years.

India has a flourishing and largely indigenous nuclear power programme and expects to have 14.6 GWe nuclear capacity on line by 2024 and 63 GWe by 2032. It aims to supply 25% of electricity from nuclear power by 2050.

Because India is outside the Nuclear Non-Proliferation Treaty due to its weapons programme, it was for 34 years largely excluded from trade in nuclear plant or materials, which has hampered its development of civil nuclear energy until 2009.

Due to earlier trade bans and lack of indigenous uranium, India has uniquely been developing a nuclear fuel cycle to exploit its reserves of thorium.

India has a vision of becoming a world leader in nuclear technology due to its expertise in fast reactors and thorium fuel cycle.

Major Non-Conventional Energy Sources

With increasing demand for energy and with fast depicting conventional sources of energy such as coal, petroleum, natural gas, etc. the non-conventional sources of energy from sun, wind, biomass, tidal energy, geo-thermal and even energy from waste material are gaining importance. This form of energy is abundant, renewable, pollution free and eco-friendly. It can be conveniently supplied to urban, rural and even remote areas. Thus, it is capable of solving the twin problems of energy supply in a decentralized manner and helping in sustaining cleaner environment. It is the energy of the future.

The disadvantage with renewable energy is that it is difficult to generate the large quantities of electricity produced by traditional fossil fuel generators. This means that we need to build more energy facilities. It also indicates that the best solution to our energy problems may be to have a balance of many different power sources.

Another disadvantage of renewable energy sources is the reliability of supply. Renewable energy often relies on the weather for its source of power. Hydro generators need rain to fill dams to supply flowing water. Wind turbines need wind to turn the blades, and solar collectors need clear skies and sunshine to collect heat and make electricity. When these resources are unavailable so is the capacity to make energy from them. This can be unpredictable and inconsistent. The current cost of renewable energy technology is also far in excess of traditional fossil fuel generation. This is because it is a new technology and as such has extremely large capital requirement. The importance of increasing the use of non-conventional or renewable power was recognized in India in the early 1970's. Four major areas of renewable energy being tapped for power generation in India are solar energy, wind energy, energy from small hydro projects and biomass.

1. **Solar Energy:** Among the various non-conventional energy resources, India possesses a very large solar energy potential; most parts of the country are blessed with good amounts of sunshine. There are about 300 clear sunny days in a year in most parts of country. In June, 2008, a National Action Plan on Climate Change was announced, which included eight major national missions with the one on solar energy being central to the mission. This

Solar panels: 4MW single axis horizontal tracker in Vellakoil Tamil Nadu

mission envisages a major step up in the utilization of solar energy for power generation and other purposes. The Jawaharlal Nehru National Solar Mission (JNNSM) was launched by the Prime Minister of India in January 2010, with a target of 20,000 MW grid solar power (based on solar thermal power generating systems and solar photovoltaic (SPV) technologies), 2000 MW of Off grid capacity including 20 million solar lighting systems and 20 million sq.m. solar thermal collector area by 2022. A Bharat Heavy Electrical Limited-made SPV battery charging system which was successfully used in the fifth Indian Antarctic stations at Dakshin Gangotri and Maitri.

2. **Wind Energy:** The wind power program is the fastest growing non-conventional energy program in India and is almost entirely coming through private sector investments. Wind electric generators of unit sizes between 225 KW and 2.10 MW have been deployed across the country. Wind Electric Generators of unit capacity up to 2.10 MW are being manufactured in India. Large profit making companies, small investors and captive users are participating in the sector. A wind generator has been installed to operate a light house at Kanai Creek Gujarat. Wind farms of a total capacity of 7.5 MW were installed in the coastal areas of Gujarat, Maharashtra, Tamil Nadu and Orissa. At Lamba in Gujarat,

Wind farm

a wind farm of 10 MW capacity, the largest in Asia, has been commissioned.

3. **Small Hydro Power:** For setting up Small Hydro Power projects attention is being focused on States with the maximum hydro potential and improving environment policies to attract private sector investments. The government also aims to develop water mills/micro hydro projects and establish local mini grids for energy security of rural region which is a step towards local power security.

4 **Biomass:** Biomass power aims at the utilization of biomass, such as agro-waste in the form of straws, stalks, stems and fibres; agro-industrial processing residues such as shells, husks, de-oiled cakes, wood from dedicated energy plantations and bagasse from sugar mills, for power generation. Using biomass to produce energy reduces the need for traditional disposal options for biomass such as landfill disposal or burning in place, while reducing dependence on fossil energy sources. The biomass process utilizes only leftover residue material as its fuel source thereby maximizing the benefits provided by the asset while minimizing the impact on the environment. Power generating systems, based on biomass combustion as well as biomass gasification, have been launched in different centres in India.

Biomass from wood

Projects have potential to meet power requirements of remote and isolated areas.

ACTIVITY

T- Chart/T-List

Aim :

- To help the student determine the salient features of the study material.
- To help them to retrieve and retain information for a longer time.

Procedure:

- The left side of the chart will have the key words of the main idea. The students can provide details to support the main idea.
- **T- Chart- Characteristic features of Nuclear Energy**

Main idea	Supporting details or examples.
Greater use of nuclear energy	1 . Concern for the environment 2. Rising prices 3. Finite nature of fossil fuels. 4. Reduce the reliance on fossil fuel for importing countries
Advantages of nuclear energy	
Disadvantages of nuclear energy	

ABUSE OF SCIENCE AND TECHNOLOGY

The influence of science on people's lives is growing. The material world that we see around us, and the way society functions today are direct manifestations of advances in science and technology. While recent benefits to humanity are unparalleled in the history of the human species, in some instances the impact has been harmful or the long-term effects give causes for serious concerns. As we move into the immediate future, quite clearly. Information Technology Environment, Nuclear Science, and Biotechnology are the areas where there have been advancements and at the same time the negative effects can also be witnessed.

1. Since the appearance of **Information Technology**, human beings have neglected each other and themselves. Today, far too many of us find ourselves in poor health, depressed, isolated, alienated, alcoholics, drug addicts, overweight, stressed out, overworked, and exhausted. We are spending less time together in f2f (face to face) conversation and interaction with our families, friends, neighbours, and colleagues and more time working, consuming, eating, drinking, driving our cars, watching TV, being online on the computer, sending emails and text messages. We have allowed this situation to evolve and have not been able, as of yet to find the strength to resist. This situation is in great need of attention and wisdom in order to find solutions for more harmony, wellness, and health for human beings everywhere, and also to set a balance between our use of technology and the time we spend in conversation and social interaction with others.

For over two thousand years the spoken word has been in the process of being colonized, first by the written word, then by the printed word, and finally by the technologized word. Now, in the Age of the Internet, computer word processing, social networking, and the text message, the spoken word is in decline and at risk of disappearing if we do not react to this evolution, which is quite rapidly disconnecting us from each other as well as from ourselves and the rich inner resources that we all possess. The only solution is to re-establish living f2f conversation and interaction by talking and listening to each other more frequently. The living spoken word heard directly and not via the media or by using a machine is an endangered form of communication which must be kept alive for the sanity and well-being of ourselves and of humanity.

2. The **environment** is another area which has sprung into prominence over the last quarter of a century. From the obvious tangible problems of a local nature, one has seen the evolution of problems of a regional nature, and then of a global nature. Ozone depletion, increase in atmospheric concentration of green house gases with possibilities of climate change and consequent hazards, destruction of bio-diversity are all examples of enormous global problems that are looming before us. The origins of these problems are created by humans. They relate to the increase of population to its present very large dimensions, and still rising, posing questions concerning the carrying capacity of the globe; and the rising tide of expectations and consumerism, particularly energy related.

Species like polar bears, seals and walruses depend on sea ice cover to breed, hunt and rest. The depleting sea ice causes malnutrition in them and their already declining population sees a further southward trend. According to Andrew Freedman, the Science Editor at Maskable, dwindling sea ice cover has forced walruses to undertake a journey of hundreds of miles for food. That's precisely why tens of thousands of them are increasingly seen on beaches in Alaska and Russia. They come here in search of rest. The polar bears use sea ice in the Arctic as a hunting ground for seals. However, they are experiencing weight loss in recent years as they have 30 less days every year to hunt on the ice.

NASA study on Arctic regions: According to a new NASA study published on an Aprii 2016 paper in Remote Sensing of Environment. Arctic regions of North America are losing their white patches and getting greener. Almost one

-third of the land cover resembles landscapes found in warmer climes. The images captured by Landsat satellites reveal a healthy growth of vegetation on the ground. The researchers are of the opinion that Quebec (Canada), western Alaska other regions became lot greener between 1984 and 2012.

Hence, the rapid loss of Arctic ice is not only+ spelling disaster for the Arctic species but also scripting a drastic shift in climatic patterns that the world is not yet ready to tackle.

3. In the area of nuclear science, the important concerns are about the development and stockpiling of nuclear weapon system with all their implications. The possibilities of nuclear war can wipe out very large parts of humanity; the proliferation of weapons of mass destruction (WMD) has become a metaphor for 21st century security concerns. Although nuclear weapons have not been used since the end of World War II, their influence on international security affairs is pervasive, and possession of WMD remains an important divide in international politics today.

   The international community knows the effects of the atom bomb and its subsequent use over Hiroshima and Nagasaki. Even in the area of peaceful uses of nuclear energy, there are great concerns about nuclear accidents, damage from nuclear radiation and the question of safe disposal of radioactive wastes.

Japan's Fukushima related cancer

In Koriyama, Japan A young woman of 21, has thyroid cancer, and wants people in her prefecture in northeastern Japan to get screened for it. She is of the 173 young people with confirmed or suspected cases since the 2011 nuclear meltdowns there, she is the first to speak out. The thyroid-cancer rate in the northern Japanese prefecture is many times higher than what is generally found, particularly among children, but the Japanese government says more cases are popping up because of rigorous screening, not the radiation that spewed from Fukushima Dai-ichi power plant. To be seen as challenging that view carries consequences in this rigidly harmony-oriented society. Even just having cancer that might be related to radiation carries a stigma in the only country to be hit with atomic bombs.

She suffers from the only disease that the medical community, including the United Nations Scientific Committee on the Effects of Atomic Radiation, has acknowledged is clearly related to the radioactive iodine that spewed into the surrounding areas after the only nuclear disaster. Though international reviews of Fukushima have predicted that cancer rates will not rise as a result of the meltdowns there, some researchers believe the prefecture's high thyroid-cancer rate is related to the accident.

4. In spite of all the benefits of genetic engineering, the threats mainly identified, are potential health risks and environment hazards. Genetic engineering and genetic modification arouses fear because one moves across species boundaries, multiplications and mutations can develop and progress rapidly in biological systems, risk assessment is much more difficult and uncertain, compared to physical engineering systems. Applications of advances in genetic engineering and cell biology arouse fear relating to human cloning.

Threats of genetic engineering

First is the concern of potential health risks. There is a possibility that introducing a gene into a plant may create a new allergen or cause an allergic reaction in susceptible individuals. For example, scientists have used lectin in potatoes to prevent aphids from attacking potato plants but some people are allergic to lectin. Also, there is a growing fear of the unknown consequences of consuming food that is not natural. Second is the environmental hazard. Environmentalists have expressed concerns over how genetically engineered food crops can affect biodiversity. For example, some pest-resistant plants are indirectly destroying harmless insects like Monarch butterflies. It is not possible to design a toxin that would only kill crop-damaging pests and remain harmless to all other insects. Hence, as more species of plants and animals become extinct, biodiversity will be lost.

Furthermore, genes may transfer to non-targeted species. For example, when the pollen of a pest-resistant crop is carried by the wind or insects to compatible natural crops, gene pollution is inevitable. This will in turn result in a loss of biodiversity.

ACTIVITY

Think Pair and Share.

Aim: To stimulate critical thinking with reference to the study material.

Procedure: The students pair in twos.

After the topic is taught the teacher gives them a cue for writing a slogan using not more than 15 to 20 words. The slogan should highlight the benefit of science and technology.

1. Science and technology are ...

The slogan can be pasted on chart paper for display in the class room.

What is important is to ensure that these advances benefit both, mankind and the environment. Biased considerations of narrow commercial interests, nationalism, fundamentalism in religious aspects and rigid ideological divides will have to give way to the basic principles of human dignity and human rights, and harmony with nature: Humane value systems that are the requirement and are need of the society, will have to be the guiding force for the application of science and technology for the benefit of all.

2 Social Structure

DIVERSITY IN INDIAN CULTURE

The term social structure points to the fact that society is structured i.e organized or arranged in particular ways. The structure of anything consists of the relatively stable interrelationship among its parts; moreover the term 'part' itself implies a certain degree of stability. There are underlying patterns and regularities, in how people behave in the society.

Sociology, as a discipline, interlinks the individual to the society. It studies smaller social units like 'family', 'clan', 'neighbourhood', etc., arguing that they contribute in building the larger society.

To illustrate, let us take the example of a building. We know that it is made up of different components such as bricks, stones, wood, glass etc. It is only when these components are arranged in an organized manner that they can create a building. Similarly, the society also has its own structure. The components of this social structure are human beings. Every human being occupies a certain position in the social structure and plays a corresponding role.

Sociology is all about the study of society, which is made up of human interactions processes and events. The human beings are group animals and within their groups in the society, they occupy statuses and perform their roles accordingly.

Our actions are often constrained by the world we live in. These constraints are put upon us due to social institutions- such as the political and economic institutions, family, marriage and kinship.

Each institution plays an important role in shaping our life and helps us to fulfil our needs. Let us discuss some of the major social institutions in this chapter.

Family

The family is the basic unit of society. It is the first and the most immediate social environment to which a child is exposed. It is in the family a child learns language, the behavioural patterns and social norms in his childhood.

Elements of Family

1. The family is a basic, definite and enduring group.
2. Family is formed by the relatively durable companionship of husband and wife.
3. Family procreates and brings up children.
4. The family can also be large in size in which persons belonging to several generations may live together.
5. The family may be limited to husband, wife or only the father and his children or only the mother and her children.

Functions of the family

The family as a social institution performs several functions.

The primary functions

Some of the functions of family are basic to its continued existence. They may also be regarded as prima functions of family. They are:

1. **Reproduction or procreation:** The process of reproduction is institutionalized in the family. Hence it assumes a regularity and stability that all societies recognize as desirable. By fulfilling its reproductive function, family has made it possible to have the propagation of species and the perpetuation of the human race.
2. **Production and rearing of the child :** The child is given protection by the family at the time of birth. Family is an institution; no other institution can as efficiently bring up the child as can the family. This can be referred to as the function of 'maintenance' also.
3. **Provision of Home :** Family provides the home for its members. The desire for home is strongly felt in men and women.
4. **Family :** An instrument of culture transmission and an Agent of Socialization:

The family guarantees not only the biological continuity of the human race but also the cultural continuity of the society of which it is a part. It transmits ideas and ideologies, folkways and mores, customs and traditions, beliefs and values from one generation to the next.

The family is an agent of social values, the morals, beliefs and ideals of society. It prepares its children for participation in larger world and acquaints them with a large culture. It is a chief agency, which prepares the new generation for life in community.

Secondary Functions of Family

In addition to the above primary functions, the family performs some secondary or non-essential functions as well. They arc-

(1) Economic Functions (2) Educational Functions (3) Religious Functions (4) The Recreational functions

1. **Economic Function :** The family fulfils the economic needs of its members. This has been the traditional function of family. Previously, the family was an economic unit. Goods were produced in the family. Members of the family used to work together in the farms for the production of goods. It was to a great extent self-sufficient. But today the situation has changed. The family members do not work together at home. They are engaged in different economic activities outside the home. Men and women contribute equally.
2. **Educational Functions :** The family provides the basis for the child's formal learning, in spite of great changes, the family still gives the child his basic training in the social attitudes and habits important to adult participation in social life. When the child grows up, he learns to manage situations outside the home and family. He extends his interests to other groups. With all this, his intelligence, his emotions, and his social habits develop until he weans himself from the original dependence on the mother, father and other family members
3. **Religious functions :** The family is a centre for the religious training of the children. The children learn from their parents various religious virtues. The family teaches the children the

religious values, moral precepts, way to worshipping God, etc. The family meets the spiritual needs of its members. It is through the family that the religious inheritance is passed on to the next generation.

4. **The Recreational Functions :** At one time, recreation was largely family based. It fostered a close solidarity. Reading aloud, hosting relatives, family reunions, singing, dancing, playing indoor games etc., brought together the entire family. The effect of this on the cohesion of the family was considerable. Recreation is now increasingly organized out side the family. Modern recreation is not designed for family - wide participation. Whether in the form of movies, sports events, plays, cricket, 'kabaddi' or tennis, it is designed for the couple or individual participation.

TYPES OR FORMS OF THE FAMILY

Sociologists have classified the family on the basis of the following factors:

1. Size
2. Residence
3. Ancestors
4. Power and Authority
5. Marriage

1. **Size :** A threefold classification can be discussed on the basis of size.

   (a) Nuclear families

(b) Extended families

(c) Joint families

In nuclear family husband, wife and their children live together. Joint families are generally big in size. They include many families and people of many generations. It possesses following features.

(a) At least three generation living together

(b) Common ancestors

(c) Common duties

2. **Residence :** On the basis of residence, family is divided into patrilocal and matrilocal families. In patrilocal families, the bride resides with the husband's family. Majority of the families is the world belongs to this type. In the matrilocal families, the bridegroom resides with the family of his wife.

3. **Inheritance :** On the basis of inheritance, the family is classified into patrilineal and matrilineal families. In the patrilineal families the inheritance is traced through the men in the family while in the matrilineal families the inheritance is traced through the woman.

4. **Power and Authority :** On the basis of power and authority, families can be divided into patriarchal and matriarchal categories. In the first type the father is the head of the family, and the familial power and authority rests in the father. In the second type of family, the familial authority lies with the mother and she is the head of family.

5. **Marriage in Indian Society :** Marriage is an important social institution. It is a relationship which is socially approved. The relationship is defined and sanctioned by custom and law. Children born of marriage are considered the legitimate offspring of the married couple. This legitimacy is important in the matter of inheritance and succession Thus marriage is not only a means of sexual gratification but also a set of cultural mechanisms to ensure the continuation of the family. It is more or less a universal social institution in India.

   Today, marriage is still considered important and necessary, and only few individuals remain unmarried by choice. Goals of marriage are, however, undergoing changes especially for the urban and educated sections of the population. The older notions regarding large size family are being replaced by preference for small-size family. Marriage for self-fulfillment rather than primarily for procreation or societal welfare is also becoming prevalent.

FORMS OF MARRIAGE

The main forms of marriage are: Polygamy and Monogamy.

Polygamy : It is the form of marriage in which either the man or the woman is married to more than one person at a time. There are two forms of polygamy. They are :

1. **Polygyny :** It is a form of marriage in which one man marries more than one woman at a given time. Polygyny is more popular than polyandry.

2. **Polyandry :** It is the marriage of one woman with more than one man. It is less common than polygyny.

Monogamy : It is a form of marriage in which one man marries one woman. It is the most common and acceptable form of marriage.

Serial monogamy : In many societies, individuals are permitted to marry again often on the death of the first spouse or after divorce but they cannot have more than one spouse at one and the same time.

RULES OF MARRIAGE

Society also prescribes certain rules pertaining to marriages. Endogamy and Exogamy that condition the marital choice.

Endogamy : It is a rule of marriage in which the life-partners are to be selected within the group. It is marriage within the group and the group may be caste, class, tribe, race, village, religious group etc. We have caste endogamy, class endogamy, sub caste endogamy, race endogamy and tribal endogamy etc. In caste endogamy marriage has to take place within the caste. Brahmin has to marry a Brahmin. In sub caste endogamy it is limited to the sub caste groups.

Exogamy : It is a rule of marriage in which an individual has to marry outside his own group. It prohibits marrying within the group. The so-called blood relatives shall neither have marital connections nor sexual contacts among themselves.

Kinship system

Man does not live alone in society. From birth till death he is surrounded by a number of people. Some of these people are his relatives, some are friends, and some are neighbours while all others are strangers and unknown to him. He is bound to all these people who are related to him either on the basis of blood or marriage. The relations based on blood or marriage may be close or distant. The bond of blood or marriage which binds people together in groups is called kinship.

Kinship system represents one of the basic social institutions. Kinship is universal and in most societies plays a significant role in the socialisation of individuals and the maintenance of group solidarity, It is supremely important in the primitive societies and extends its influence on almost all their activities - social, economic, political, religious, etc.

RULE OF DESCENT

1. **Patrilineal Descent :** According to this rule, descent is traced through the father's or men line. Here the descent criterion is restricted to males, and only descendants of a common ancestor the male line will be recognised as kin. These are known as agnatic or patrilineal kin.

2. **Matrilineal Descent :** Here the descent of the individual is traced through the mother or female exclusively. The descendants are called here uterine or matrilineal kin.

   These two modes of tracing the descent are called "unilineal", that, they select one "line" either the male or female. These principles or rules are not necessarily mutually exclusive within society.

3. **Bilateral Descent :** This is a rule in which the descent is traced

through both the lines or female line and also the male line for some or the other purpose.

What is important here is that almost all kinship systems recognise 'bilateral' relationship that is relationships to both maternal and paternal kins.

Importance of the Rule of Descent

The rule of descent is very important for two main reasons;

1. Rule of descent establishes for every individual a network of social positions in which participates. He comes to know about his obligations and rights.
2. Rule of descent invariably defines some rights of inheritance. Inheritance and succession would go normally along the line of descent.

TYPES OF KINSHIP

Kinship is of two types:

1. Affinal Kinship, and
2. Consanguineous Kinship

1. **Affinal Kinship :** The bond of marriage is called 'affinal' kinship. When a person marries, he establishes relationship not only with the girl whom he marries but also with a number of other people in the girl's family. Moreover, it is not only the person marrying who gets bound to the family members of the girl, but his family members also get bound to the family members of the girl. Thus, a host of relations are created as

soon as a marriage takes place. For examples, after marriage a person becomes not only a husband but he also becomes brother-in-law and son- in-law.

2. **Consanguineous Kinship :** The bond of blood is called consanguineous kinship. The consanguineous kin are related through blood whereas the affinal kin are related through marriage. The bond between parents and their children and that between parents and their children and that between parents and their children and that between siblings is consanguineous kinship. Siblings are the children of the same parents. Thus, son, brother, sister, uncle (chacha), elder uncle (tau) nephew and cousin are consanguineous kin, i.e. related through blood.

DEGREE OF KINSHIP

On the basis of nearness of distance relatives can be classified in several categories.

Primary Kins : Some relatives are very close, direct and near, for example, father, son, sister-brother, husband-wife. They are called primary kin.

Secondary Kins : They are related through primary kin. They are not our primary kin but are the primary kin of our primary kin, hence our secondary kin. For example, father's brother (chacha), sister, husband (bahnoi) are secondary kin. The father is my primary kin and his brother is the primary kin of father. Therefore, father's brother is my secondary kin, the primary kin of primary kin. Similarly, sister is my primary kin but her husband is my secondary kin.

Tertiary Kins : They are secondary kin of our primary kin and the primary kin of our secondary kin. Thus the wife of brother-in-law (sala) called sarhaj in Hindi, is tertiary kin because brother-in-law is my secondary kin and his wife is the primary kin of brother- in-law similarly, the brother-in-law of my brother is my tertiary kin because the brother is my primary kin and his the brother-in-law is the secondary kin of my brother.

SOCIAL STRATIFICATION

To be more clear about social structure and to understand the concept better, we need to understand the concept of social stratification. In sociology and anthropology, social stratification is the hierarchical arrangement of social classes, castes and strata within a society. While these hierarchies are not universal to all societies, they are the norm among state-level cultures (as distinguished from hunter-gatherers or other social arrangements). The term stratification is derived from the geological concept of strata, or rock layers created by natural processes.

UNDERSTANDING THE SYSTEMS OF STRATIFICATION

Ever since people first began to speculate about the nature of human society, there have been differences between individuals and groups within society.

The term social inequality describes a condition in which members of society have different amounts of wealth, prestige, or power. Some degree of social inequality characterizes every society. When a system of social inequality is based on a hierarchy of groups, sociologists refer to it as stratification: a structured ranking of entire groups of people that perpetuates unequal economic rewards and power in a society.

Stratification involves the ways in which one generation passes on social inequalities to the next, producing groups of people arranged in rank order, from low to high.

Some of the systems of stratification have been explained in this chapter.

CASTE

'Many of us, I dare say, have witnessed local, national or international expositions of material objects that make up the sum total of human civilization. But few can entertain the idea of there being such a thing as an exposition of human institutions. Exhibition of human institutions is a strange idea; some might call it the wildest of ideas. But as students of Ethnology I hope you will not be hard on this innovation, for it is not so, and to you at least it should not be strange.'

Dr B.R Ambedkar, CASTES IN INDIA: Their Mechanism, Genesis and Development

The term 'caste' comes from the Portuguese 'caste' meaning, 'race' or 'pure stock'. There are many words which are used to denote caste, such as 'varna' and 'jati'. The Varna consists of four categories, each ranked differently in terms of social honour. The jati are locally defined groups within which the caste ranks are organized.

The caste system was extremely elaborate and varied in its structure from area to area. Those in the highest varna, the Brahmins, represented the most elevated condition of purity, followed by Kshatriyas, the warrior caste, Vaisya, the traders and the Shudras, the lowest.

Characteristics of the Caste System

1. **Caste is ascribed :** A man is born into his/her caste. He/She dies in the same caste in which he is born and it is the caste that determines his status in life.
2. **Restriction on Food Habits :** The second element of caste is its prescription of certain kinds of food for different castes. For instance, a Brahmin is not permitted to eat non-vegetarian food. Kshalriyas and Vaishyas are also forbidden to take certain kinds of foods as beef, but Shudras have the liberty to consume any type of food.
3. **Caste is Endogamous :** Endogamy is the most important element of caste system. According to this, each one must marry within his own caste and within the sub-group if there be any in that caste. The system has become so rigid that inter-caste marriages have become too difficult, because two persons belonging to two different castes differ in food habits, cultural habits etc. The violation of the rule of endogamy i.e. marrying outside the caste would mean ostracism and loss of caste.
4. **Hierarchical Social Structure :** The caste structure of the society is hierarchy or system of subordination held together by the relations of superiority and inferiority at the apex of

which are Brahmins and at the lowest rung are the Shudras. The relative position that a person occupies in the caste hierarchy is mostly determined by its relations to the Brahmins. Thus, the highest caste is that from whom a Brahmin will accept food. The next is that caste from whom the three castes Brahmins, Kahatriyas and Vaishyas (regarded as twice born) may accept food. At the lowest are those castes from whom the higher castes cannot accept any food or drink, and at times not even be touched for the fear of contamination-hence in this hierarchy the Brahmins enjoy a number of social and religious privileges while at the same time they have suffered a series of setbacks.

Members of a particular caste are expected to follow the caste occupation. The abandonment of heredity occupation is not thought to be right. No caste would allow its members to take to any occupation which was either degrading. Some occupations are considered to be superior and sacred while certain others degrading and inferior. For a long time, occupations were very much associated with the caste system. Each caste had its own specific occupation. The caste members were expected to continue the same occupations. Occupations were almost hereditary. Individual talents, aptitudes, interests, enterprise, abilities, and achievements were neglected. But agriculture, trade and labour in the field were thrown open to all the castes. At the same time, no caste would allow its members to take up to any profession, which was either degrading or impure.

Role of Caste Today

The role played by caste has changed in the recent times.

Besides industrialisation and urbanisation, other factors such as Westernisation, Sanskritisation, reorganisation of Indian states, spread of education, socio-religious reforms, spatial and occupational mobility and growth of market economy have greatly affected the caste system.

1. **Increase in the Organisational Power of Caste**

   Education makes people liberal, broad-minded, rationale and democratic. Educated people arc believed to be less conservative and superstitious. Hence it was expected that with the growth of literacy in India, caste mindedness and casteism would come down. On the contrary, in some cases caste-consciousness of the members has been found to be increasing. Every caste wants to safeguard its interests. For fulfilling the purpose, in some places, castes are getting themselves organised on the model of labour unions.

2. **Political Role of Caste**

   Caste and politics have come to affect each other now. Caste has become an inseparable aspect of our politics. In fact, it is tightening its hold on politics. Elections are fought more often on the basis of caste. Selection of candidates, voting analysis, selection of legislative party leaders, distribution of ministerial portfolios etc., are very much based on caste. Even the communist parties which project the ideal of a casteless and classless society are also not an exception to this. Politics of each state, as M.N. Srinivas says, is virtually the politics of confrontation of its "dominant castes" Thus, unless one knows the political confrontation between the dominant castes such as Ligayats and Vokkaligas in Karnataka and Reddys and Kammas in Andhra Pradesh, one cannot understand the politics of these two states. M.N. Srinivas also makes a distinction between caste at the ritual level and caste at the political level. Caste at the ritual level is smaller unit than the caste at the political level.

3. **Protection for Scheduled Castes and other Backward Classes**

   The Constitution of India has made enough provisions to protect the interests of Scheduled Castes and Tribes. They are offered more political, educational and service opportunities through the reservation policy, seats are reserved for them from Mandal panchayat to Parliament and in all government departments. Though the reservation policy is against the declared goal of establishment of a casteless society, all political parties have supported it mostly, for political purposes. According to M.N, Srinivas, "The provision of constitutional safeguards to..,. Scheduled Castes and Tribes has given a new lease of life to caste," These provisions have made some of them develop vested interests to reap permanently the benefits of reservation. They are also tempting many other castes to bring pressure on the government to declare them as belonging to the category of Scheduled Castes.

4. **Sanskritisation and Westernisation**

   As M.N. Srinivas has pointed out, two important trends are witnessed in caste - the process of 'Sanskritisation' and that of 'Westernisation'. The former refers to a process in which the lower castes tend to imitate the values, practices and other life-styles of some dominant upper castes. The latter denotes a process in which the upper-caste people tend to mould their life-styles on the model of Westerners.

5. **Backward Classes Movement**

The non-Brahmin castes today are getting themselves more and more organised to challenge the supremacy of the Brahmins and to assert their rights. The establishment of 'Satyashodhak Samaj' by Jyotirao Phooley in Poona in 1873 marked the beginning of such a non- Brahmin movement. This movement against the Brahmin supremacy by the lower castes came to be known as Backward Classes Movement, In the beginning, the main aim of this movement was to limit the Brahmin monopoly in the two fields such as education and appointment to government posts.

The Backward Classes Movement has become a vital political force today. Its influence has changed the political scenario of the country. This movement has made the Brahmins politically weak and insignificant especially in Kerala and Tamil Nadu. This movement has also brought pressure on different political parties to create special opportunities for the lowest caste people enabling them to come up to the level of other higher castes. Due to this pressure, Backward Classes Commissions were established at Central and State levels which recommended "reservation" for backward castes/classes.

6. **Competitive Role of Castes**

Mutual interdependence of castes, which existed for centuries and was reinforced by the institutional system of "jajmani", is not found today. As M.N. Srinivas points out, the "vertical solidarity" of castes has been replaced by "horizontal solidarity". "Live and let live" policy, which was once associated with the caste makes no sense today. On the contrary, some times, each caste looks at the other with suspicion, contempt, and jealousy and finds in it a challenger, a competitor. Excessive caste-mindedness and caste-patriotism have added to this competition. The economic base of a caste and its hold over the political power virtually determine the intensity of this competitiveness. This competitive spirit further strengthens caste-mindedness.

ACTIVITY

Have you ever seen matrimonial advertisements? Divide your class into groups and look at different newspapers, magazines and the internet. Discuss your findings. Do you think endogamy is still the prevalent norm? How does it help you to understand choice in marriage? More importantly, what kind of changes in society does it reflect?

In a few suspected cases of honour killing, young men and women faced a violent end for marrying outside their own cast and community. However there has been social progress in society and we have seen inter-caste, inter community and inter-religious marriages on the rise which have been accepted in society.

TRIBE

India is the home to large number of indigenous people, who are still untouched by the lifestyle of the modem world. With more than 84.4 million, India has the largest population of the tribal people in the world. These tribal people also known as the 'adivasis' are the poorest in the country, who are still dependent on hunting, agriculture and fishing. Some of the major tribal groups in India include Gonds, Santhals, Khasis, Angamis, Bhils, Bhutias and Great Andamanese. All these tribal people have their own culture, tradition, language and lifestyle. This enables the tourist to get an insight into many different cultures at the same time on the tribal tour to India.

In general tribal population is expected to possess some of the following characteristics:

1. Tribes have their roots in the soil dating back to a very early period.
2. They live in relative isolation in the hills and forests.
3. They need to be socially and economically developed.,
4. In terms of their cultural ethos (language, institutions, beliefs and customs), their life style is very different from the other section of society.

Tribes are the descendents from a country's aboriginal population and today they are completely or partly deprived of the rights of their own territory. Indigenous peoples are strikingly different and diverse in their culture, religion, social and economic organisations.

CLASSIFICATION OF TRIBES

Tribes have been classified according to their 'permanent' and 'acquired' traits.

Permanent Traits

1. **Region :** Tribal population is widely spread. About 85% of the tribal population lives in middle India, a wide band stretching from Gujarat and Rajasthan in the west to West Bengal and Orissa in the east, with Madhya Pradesh, Jharkhand, Chattisgarh and parts of Maharashtra and Andhra Pradesh forming the heart of this region.
2. **Language :** Tribes have been categorized into 4 categories. 1% of the population speaks Indo-Aryan, 3% of the population speaks Dravidian. Almost all tribals speak Austric and over 80% speak Tibeto-Burman.
3. **Race :** They are classified as Negrito, Australoid, Mongoloid, Dravidian and Aryan categories.
4. **Size :** The biggest tribes are Gonds, Bhils, Oraons, Minas, Bodos and Mundas.

Acquired Traits

Classification here is based on two main criteria-

1. **Mode of livelihood :** Tribes are categorized into fishermen, food gatherers and hunters, shifting cultivators, peasants and plantation and industrial workers.
2. **Degree of assimilation into the mainstream society:** Assimilation can be seen from the point of view of the tribes

or from the point of view of the dominant mainstream. From tribes point of view, the attitude of the dominant section of the society is taken into consideration. There are some tribes, which are inclined towards joining the mainstream society whereas there are some who oppose it completely. From the mainstream point of view, some tribes are given a high status in the society whereas some have been accorded low status.

Scheduled Tribes

The Constitution of India, Anicle 366 (25) defines Scheduled Tribes as "such tribes or tribal communities or part of or groups within such tribes or tribal communities as are deemed under Article 342 to the scheduled Tribes (STs) for the purposes of this Constitution". In Article 342, the procedure to be followed for specification of a scheduled tribe is prescribed. However, it does not contain the criterion for the specification of any community as scheduled tribe. An often-used criterion is based on attributes such as:

- Geographical isolation - they live in cloistered, exclusive, remote and inhospitable areas such as hills and forests.
- Backwardness - their livelihood is based on primitive agriculture, a low-value closed economy with a low level of technology that leads to their poverty. They have low levels of literacy and health.
- Distinctive culture, language and religion - communities have developed their own distinctive culture, language and religion.
- Shyness of contact - they have a marginal degree of contact with other cultures and people.

- Tribal people constitute 8.6% of the India's total population. Northeastern states like Assam, Meghalaya, Tripura, Arunachal Pradesh, Mizoram, Manipur, and Nagaland have a tribal population of more than 90%. Some of the major tribal groups in India include Gonds, Santhals, Khasis, Angamis, Bhils, Bhutias and Great Andamanese. All these tribal people have their own culture, tradition, language and lifestyle.

Tribes in India Today

Tribes are becoming conscious, both socially and politically, of maintaining and preserving their ethnic mid cultural identity and also of protecting themselves against exploitation by outsiders. In newly formed states like Chattisgarh and Jharkhand with majority of the population consisting of tribes, there is a new tribal identity, which has been carved. However, they are still not completely incorporated into the mainstream society and face a lot of problems like their resources being taken away.

The 'assimilationist model of the tribes' integration with non-tribal India demands structural linkages of the tribes with the non-tribes. The 'isolationist' model would not be much relevant today in the face of rapid changes in Indian society.

Despite vast changes taking place in India, tribal consciousness has been strengthened mainly to project tribes as distinct components of Indian society. Industrialisation in Jharkhand, for example, has promoted both tribal consciousness and integration with the non-tribal sections in the region. The demand for autonomy by tribals has originated from their fear of loss of cultural autonomy and of exploitation.

SOCIAL CLASS IN INDIA

A class system is a social ranking based primarily on economic position in which achieved characteristics can influence social mobility. In contrast to slavery and caste systems, the boundaries between classes are imprecisely defined, and one can move from one stratum, or level, of society to another. Class systems maintain stable stratification hierarchies and patterns of class divisions, and they, too, are marked by unequal distribution of wealth and power.

Caste and class are two principles of stratification which age persisted in the Indian social systems in a dialectical relationship.

The sociology of Indian class stratification should not only take into account the present day processes among the various class strata but also analyse them in the historical contexts of change. Studies which throw light on the class structure and its processes in the traditional Indian society reveal that class structure was related to the modes of production and ownership.

Kings, feudal chiefs, traders, artisans, peasants, labourers and the social relationships of these groups are important for understanding the Indian class structure.

The king occupied the highest position with so many loyalties and vassals and his subjects owed allegiance to him and in turn the king was responsible for the welfare of his people. The merchants, the business class, were the most mobile. Here, wealth and economic factors played important roles in determining one's class position; and in that context one's social position based on caste became weakened. The establishment of various economic and political institutions by the British enhanced the mobility of these groups of people so that they could mobilise economic surpluses from village to towns and cities.

Sociologist Karl Marx examined social relations within capitalism -an economic system in which the means of production are held largely in private hands and the main incentive for economic activity is the accumulation of profits. The bourgeoisie or capitalist class, owns the means of production, such as factories and machinery; the proletariat is the working class. According to Marx, exploitation of the proletariat will inevitably lead to the destruction of the capitalist system, because the workers will revolt. But first, the working class needs to develop class consciousness-a subjective awareness of common vested interests and the need for collective political action to bring about social change. Often, workers must overcome false consciousness or an attitude held by members of a class that does not accurately reflect their objective position.

REGIONALISM, COMMUNALISM, SECULARISM

India is a pluralistic society and its unity has been threatened a number of times from forces in the shape of communalism, secularism and regionalism.

COMMUNALISM

Communalism is an ideological concept, which states that society is divided into religious communities whose interest differ and are, at times, even opposed to each other. The antagonism practiced by the people of one community against the people of other community and religion can be termed as 'communalism'.

Growth of Communalism: Causes

Jawaharlal Nehru once described communalism as the Indian version of fascism. He said, while all communalism is bad, we must remember that minority communalism is born out of fear, while majority communalism takes the form of political reaction to assert dominance. But he added: 'there could be no compromise on the issue of communalism, Hindu communalism or Muslim communalism, as it is a challenge to Indian nationhood and Indian nationalism.' The main forces, which have encouraged the growth of communalism in contemporary India, are;

1. **Orthodoxy :** The orthodox members of minorities feel that they have a distinct entity with their own cultural pattern, personal laws and thought. There are strong elements of conservatism and fundamentalism amongst various religious sects. Such feeling has prevented them from accepting the concept of secularism and religious tolerance.
2. **Design of the Leaders :** Communalism has flourished in India because some communal minded religious leaders desire to flourish it in the interest of their own communities. The demand for separate electorate and the organization of Muslim league were the practical manifestations of this line of thought. The British rule which produced the divide and rule policy, separate electorate on the basis of religion strengthened the basis of communalism in India. Ultimately the partition

of the country into India and Pakistan provided further an antagonistic feeling towards each other.

3. **Weak Economic Status :** Some groups in India have failed to adopt the scientific and technological education. Due to their educational backwardness, they have not been represented sufficiently in the public service, industry and trade. This causes the feeling of relative deprivation and such feelings contain the seeds of communalism.

4. **Social Causes :** Cultural similarity is a powerful factors in fostering amicable relations between any two social groups. But the social institutions, customs and practices of Hindus and Muslims are so divergent that they think themselves to be two distinct communities.

5. **Psychological Causes:** Psychological factors play an important role in the development of communalism. The Hindus think that the Muslims are fanatics and fundamentalists. They also believe that Muslims are unpatriotic. On the contrary, the Muslims feel that they are being treated as second rate citizens in India and their religious beliefs and practices are considered inferior. These feelings lead to communal ill-feeling.

6. **Provocation of Enemy Countries :** Some foreign countries try to destabilize our country by setting one community against the other through their agents. Pakistan has played a role in fostering communal feeling among the Muslims of our country. Pakistan has been encouraging and promoting communal riots by instigating the militant sections of Indian

Muslim community. Kashmir youths are trained by Pakistan to destabilize India's internal security by spreading communal venom.

ACTIVITY

Talk to your parents and the elders in your family and collect from them poems, songs, short stories which highlight issues such as religious pluralism syncretism or communal harmony. When you have collected all this material and presented them in class, you may be pleasantly surprised to learn how broad based our traditions of religious pluralism are and how widely they are shared across different linguistic groups, regions and religions.

7. **Negative Impact of Mass Media :** The messages relating to communal tension or riot in any part of the country spread through the mass media. This results in further tension and riots between two rival religious groups.

The small insecure communities always look to government or move towards communal parties for protection. The Pundits in Kashmir, the innocent victims of communal riots in Mumbai, Uttar Pradesh, Gujarat and other states, and the sufferers of violence of extremists in Bihar, Assam, look towards the secular state of India for the security of life and property.

A train burning during the communal riots in Gujarat in 2002

SECULARISM

"I do not expect India of my dreams to develop one religion, i.e., to be wholly Hindu or wholly Christian or wholly Mussalman, but I want it to be wholly

tolerant, with its religions working side by side with one another." So said Mahatma Gandhi.

Secularism, along with a commitment to the ideals of democracy, equality and freedom were some of the fundamental principles that inspired a large section of our people to fight against British colonialism. After independence, these values were enshrined in the Constitution, thus enjoining the state to uphold these principles.

MEANING AND DEFINITION

In the west, secularism was part of a whole range of new ideas and institutions that marked the end of the feudal order and the emergence of a sovereign modern nation-state with new forms of economic organisation. It arose from the west, however today it need not limit its application to other cultures. Modern western secularism was the consequence of the search for a way out of religious wars (often between Christians of various persuasions) and the need to separate the domain of the state from that of the Church.

Secularism has become essential for modem democratic nation-states to ensure a strong sense of identification with the polity based on a common sense of identity, where being a citizen takes precedence over all other identities like family, race, class and religion.

Apart from implying a separation of the Church from the state, it also suggests freedom to the individual. The enlightenment in Europe heralded a new era where reason rather than religion, became the guiding factor for all aspects of human life. Secular concerns, it came to be argued, are of this world and religion which is concerned with the unknown world was to be kept away from this. However, this did not necessarily imply a hostile relationship between the two, only that both are exclusive.

In sharp contrast with this position is the one that sees religion and secularism as being fundamentally opposed to one another, in the sense that the continued presence of religion in a society indicates its backwardness and that ultimately, human progress and prosperity, and the creation of a truly egalitarian society is possible only in the absence of religion.

In India, secularism is popularly understood as the best philosophy that would enable people belonging to diverse religious backgrounds to live together in a harmonious manner, and create a state that would accord the

Challenges and Threats to Secularism in India

Secularism in practice it is not so easy to follow. In India, there is deep religious sentiment prevailing among its different religious communities.

In India, backwardness in the form of illiteracy, ignorance, poverty, population explosion and environmental pollution - prevails in the country in alarming proportions. Such factors result in hostility and tension amongst public, leading to communal undercurrents.

Today, the biggest challenge to the Indian nation is coming from forces claiming to represent a particular religion. There is an emergency of extremist voices that claim to speak for their religion and they are laying down demands that threaten the very idea of a secular India.

REGIONALISM

Meaning

Regionalism is a feeling or an ideology among a section of people residing in a particular geographical space characterized by unique language, culture etc., that they are the sons of the soil and every opportunity in their land must be given to them first but not to the outsiders.

Growth and Development

Regionalism in India can be traced back to Dravidan Movement started in Tamil Nadu. The movement initially focused on empowering Dalits, non-Brahmins, and poor people. Later it turned against imposition of Hindi as sole official language on non-Hindi speaking areas. The movement slowly declined and today they have become prominent regional parties after many splits and factionalism.

Throughout India, regionalism persisted with an aim for demand for a separate state– for example, in Assam ULFA militants and Khalistan movement in Punjab.

It can be traced that regionalism slowly turned from non-violent means to violent means to achieve their goals. From Potti Sriramulu's non-violent means of fasting to ULFA's violent means, regionalism has come a long way.

Regionalism in contemporary India is readily used for political gains by petty politicians and other organizations.

When violence is used against people in the name of regionalism, it is a criminal act and is punishable.

ACTIVITY

Find out about the origins of your own State. When was it formed? What were the main criteria used to define it?- Was it language, ethnic/tribal identity, regional deprivation, ecological difference or other criterion? How does this compare with other State of India in terms of the criteria for their formation? Are you aware of any current social movements that are demanding the creation of a State? Try to find out the criteria being used by these movements [Hint: Check the Telengana and Vidarbha movements and others in your region.]

The resurgence of regionalism in various parts of the country has emerged as such a serious problem that it threatens to divide the country. The creation of new states like Jharkhand, Uttaranchal (Uttarakhand) and Chhattisgarh in recent times is in fact the expression of territorial regionalism. Again, the demand for Bodoland, Vidarbha, Telangana, Gorkhaland, etc. can be traced in the earnest desire of the people to have their regional identity, which results from regional imbalances. In fact, it is the natural desire of the people in a region or territory to make rapid social and economic development so that they may live happily. But in course of time when some part of the region makes rapid development, and other remains neglected, then the feelings of anger and frustration creep into the mind of the people which find expression in demand for a separate homeland. Thus, this development imbalance in which some part of the state receives special attention and other areas are neglected and allowed to rot causing immense suffering and hardship to the common appeared in the form of Gorkha movement, Bodo movement, Telangana movement, etc.

The effort in this chapter has been to understand India's social structure and the various layers of the society. India is a diverse country and in order to understand its structure, it is very important to know about the diverse groups and issues, which threaten this diversity and unity.

QUESTIONS

1. What is a social structure? Enlist some of its features.
2. Discuss the various form of social stratification in India
3. What are the different senses in which 'secularism' has been understood in India?
4. What is regionalism? What factors is it usually based on?
5. What role does caste play in the present society?
6. How did Karl Marx explain 'class'?

3 Protection of Environment

INTRODUCTION

In recent years mankind's consciousness has been aroused strongly towards environmental protection and ecological preservation. It is of utmost importance that people should be aware, not only of the challenges involved but also of the role to be played by each individual in protecting the environment.

Air, water and land are the basic requirements of life. However, overpopulation and rapid industrialization has caused destruction of the environment. Man has continuously tampered with nature resulting in increased threat to his life due to the polluted air, lack of potable water and the imbalance established in the biosphere.

Thus, while developing technologies for the benefit of man, it is also essential for us to study, simultaneously, their impact on the environment, so that the processes which the nature has devised for conservation of resources, are not affected.

ENVIRONMENT

The word environment is derived from the word 'environ' which means surrounding. Our surroundings include abiotic factors such as light, air, water, soil, etc. and biotic factors like human beings, plants, animals, microbes etc. The environment is a composite of many variables, which surrounds man as well as other living organisms. The environment encompasses the interrelationships which exist among and between water, air and land and human beings and other living creatures such as plants, animals and micro organisms.

ENVIRONMENTAL POLLUTION

Environmental pollution has existed for centuries but only started to be significant following the industrial revolution in 19th century. Today, environmental pollution is one of the main threats for our planet. Pollution destroys the living environment and endangers human existence on earth. The economy does find many benefits in technological development; however, toxic emissions due to the work of factories, transportation, and construction sites pollute the environment substantially.

Pollution occurs when the natural environment cannot destroy an element without creating harm or damage to itself. The elements involved are not produced by nature, and the process of destruction can vary from a few days to thousands of years. Pollution must be taken seriously, as it has a negative effect on natural elements that are needed for life to exist on earth, such as air, water and land.

TYPES OF POLLUTION

Air Pollution

Air pollution may be defined as the presence of one or more contaminants like dust, mist, smoke or colour in the atmosphere, that are injurious to human beings, plants and animals. It is the quantity or concentration of a chemical in the air that makes the difference between it being 'harmless' and 'polluting'.

ACTIVITY

Word Scramble

Aim

- To identify key words.
- To associate the key words with the context.

Procedure

Teacher identifies section from the chapter and asks the students to identify key words that assimilate the portion taught. On a lighter note the teacher gives them a word scramble made of the key words.

Word Scramble: Unscramble the words below:

1. iennvrmoent ....
2. ttizriaouasindiln ....
3. tiocsrtuden ....
4. loitolupn ....
5. sue siflfol ....
6. nyeloeaozr ....
7. ioismesn ....
8. orbcflaooouhclorrn ....
9. rtarifoeegrr ....
10. nsahogeesegrues ....

Answers: ozone layer, environment, fossil fuel, chlorofluorocarbon. refrigerator, Industrialization, destruction, pollution, emission, greenhouse gases

Natural Air Pollution: Some types of air pollution are caused naturally. For example– forest fires, dust storms, erupting volcanoes, and gases released from radioactive decay of rocks inside earth.

Causes of Air Pollution by Man's Activities

1. **Burning of fossil fuels:** Smoke emitting from vehicles cause immense amount of pollution. Carbon monoxide caused by improper or incomplete combustion and generally emitted

from vehicles is a major pollutant. Sulphur dioxide emitted from the combustion of fossil fuels like coal, petroleum and other factory combustibles is also another major cause of air pollution. There are many harmful gases that are emitted in the atmosphere and are injurious to health and environment.

2. **Exhaust from factories, industries and refineries:** Manufacturing industries release large amount of carbon monoxide, hydrocarbons, organic compounds, and chemicals into the air, depleting the quality of air.

3. **Agricultural activities:** Use of insecticides, pesticides and fertilizers in agricultural activities has grown quite a lot. They emit harmful chemicals into the air and can also cause water pollution.

4. **Mining operations:** Mining is a process wherein minerals from below the earth are extracted using large equipment. During the process, dust and chemicals are released in the air causing enormous air pollution. This is one of the reasons responsible for the deterioriating health conditions of workers and nearby residents.

5. **Indoor air pollution:** Household cleaning products, painting supplies and many other gadgets emit toxic chemicals in the air and cause air pollution.

Traffic jams result in air pollution

Air pollution

Effects of Air Pollution

1. **Health problems:** People exposed to high levels of certain air pollutants may experience irritation of the eyes, nose, and throat, wheezing, coughing, chest tightness, and breathing difficulties. In addition, long-term exposure to air pollution can cause cancer and damage to the immune, neurological, reproductive, and respiratory systems.
2. **Global warming:** Another direct effect that the world is witnessing is global warming due to increase in the concentration of green house gases. With increased temperatures, there is increase in sea levels due to the melting of icebergs, leading to the fear of displacement and loss of habitat.
3. **Depletion of ozone layer:** The earth's ozone layer is depleting due to the presence of chlorofluorocarbons, and hydro chlorofluorocarbons in the atmosphere. As ozone layer will become thin, it will emit harmful rays back on earth and can cause skin and eye related problems and also destruction of the ecosystem.
4. **Effect on wildlife:** Animals also face the effect of air pollution. Toxic chemicals present in the air can force wildlife species to move to new place and change their habitat. The toxic pollutants over the surface of the water can affect marine life.
5. **Crop and forest damage:** Crop and forest damage can also result from acid rain and from increased UV radiation caused by ozone depletion.
6. **Acid rain:** Precipitation containing harmful gases released into

the atmosphere when fossil fuels are burned is known as acid rain. These acids fall to the earth as wet precipitation (rain, snow, or fog). This precipitation causes soil and water bodies to acidify, making the water unsuitable for wildlife and aquatic life.

Measures to Control Air Pollution

The atmosphere has several in-built self cleaning processes such as dispersion, gravitational settling, absorption, rain-washout, etc to cleanse the atmosphere. However, control of contaminants at their source level is desirable by preventive or control technologies. Some measures that can be adopted in this direction are:

1. Using unleaded petrol and fuels with low sulphur and ash content.
2. Encouraging people to walk, use public transport, or use a cycle as opposed to private vehicles.
3. Ensure that houses, schools, restaurants and playgrounds are not located on busy streets.
4. Plant trees along busy streets because they absorb carbon dioxide and reduce noise level.
5. Continuous monitoring of the atmosphere for pollutants should be carried out to know the emission levels.
6. Industries and waste disposal sites should be situated outside the city.
7. Emission rates should be restricted to permissible levels by each and every industry.

8. Incorporation of air pollution control equipment in design of plant layout must be made mandatory.

OZONE DEPLETION

Stratospheric ozone filters out most of the sun's potentially harmful shortwave ultraviolet (UV) radiation. If ozone gets depleted- then more UV rays will reach the earth. Exposure to higher amounts of UV radiation could have serious impacts on human beings, animals and plants such as skin cancer, sunburn, premature aging of the skin, cataracts, blindness. It can have adverse impact on the ecosystems as well. Several of the world's major crop species are particularly vulnerable to increased UV, resulting in reduced growth, photosynthesis and flowering. Planktons (tiny organisms in the surface layer of oceans) are threatened by increased UV radiation. Decreases in plankton could disrupt the fresh and saltwater food chains.

Scientific evidence indicates that stratospheric ozone is being destroyed by a group of manufactured chemicals, containing chlorine and bromine. These chemicals are called "ozone-depleting substances" (ODS). ODS are very stable, nontoxic and environmentally safe in the lower atmosphere, which is why they became so popular in the first place. However, their very stability allows them to float up, intact, to the stratosphere. Once there, they are broken apart by the intense ultraviolet light, releasing chlorine and bromine. Chlorine and bromine demolish ozone at an alarming rate, by stripping an atom from the ozone molecule. A single molecule of chlorine can break apart thousands of molecules of ozone. Furthermore, ODS have a long lifetime in our atmosphere — up to several centuries. This means most of the ODS we've released over the last 80 years are still making their way to the stratosphere, where they will add to the ozone destruction.

The main Ozone-Depleting Substances (ODS): Chlorofluorocarbons (CFCs) are most widely used ODS, accounting for over 80% of total stratospheric ozone depletion. They are used as coolants in refrigerators, freezers and air conditioners in buildings etc. They are also found in industrial solvents, dry-cleaning agents and foam products. To prevent further ozone depletion we should buy refrigerators, freezers, vehicle, air conditioners and vehicles with models that do not use CFC.

Hydro fluorocarbons (HFCs) are being developed to replace CFCs and HCFCs, for use in vehicle air conditioning. HFCs do not deplete ozone, but they are strong greenhouse gases. Thus HFCs are still a better option until safer substitutes are discovered.

GREENHOUSE EFFECT

The greenhouse effect is a natural process that warms the earth's surface. When the sun's energy reaches the earth's atmosphere, some of it is reflected back to space and the rest is absorbed and re-radiated by greenhouse gases. Greenhouse gases include water vapour, carbon dioxide, methane, nitrous oxide, ozone and some artificial chemicals such as Chlorofluorocarbons (CFCs).

The absorbed energy warms the atmosphere and the surface of the earth. This process maintains the earth's temperature allowing life to exist. Due to excessive presence of some gasses in the atmosphere, escape of heat from earth surface is prevented, resulting in heating of earth called 'global warming'.

Enhanced Greenhouse Effect

Human activities - particularly burning of fossil fuels (coal, oil and natural gas), agriculture and land clearing - are all increasing the concentrations of greenhouse gases. The harmful effects of greenhouse gasses are global warming, climate change, ozone depletion, sea level rise, adverse effects on biodiversity etc.

Solution to Delhi's pollution problem

A recent survey revealed that air pollution in Delhi is one-and-a-half times worse than in Beijing. The National Capital's pollution troubles have prompted proposals such as the Odd-Even Formula and a plan to disallow new diesel vehicles on the streets of Delhi.

There are several solutions if the government wishes to have a lasting and sustainable solution to urban chaos. Steps to decongest city roads and improve quality needs to be taken hand in hand because one feeds on another. Odd-even transport sorting, used under emergency situations in Paris, Beijing and other cities globally, is just one of them. Along with such drastic measures to ration road space, the government needs to improve public transport, enforce stricter emission norms and also tone up modes of transport such as three-wheelers and taxi.

Along with all this, here are a few steps that need urgent attention if we are serious about decongesting Indian cities:

- Invest in developing pedestrian infrastructure
- Make a plan for last mile connectivity
- Develop pedestrian zones in city centres and shopping areas
- Zero tolerance for on-street parking
- Hike parking charges

WATER POLLUTION

Water pollution is any chemical, physical or biological change in the quality of water that has a harmful effect on living things that drinks, lives in water or uses it. Thus, water pollution is the contamination of water bodies like ocean, river, lake and pond.

Causes of Water Pollution

Untreated sewage contaminates the stream

Any human activity can have an effect on the quality of the water environment. When farmers fertilize the fields, the chemicals they use are gradually washed by rain into the groundwater or surface waters nearby. Chemicals released by smokestacks (chimneys) can enter the atmosphere and then fall back to earth as rain, entering seas, rivers, and lakes and causing water pollution. Water pollution has many different causes and this is one of the reasons why it is such a difficult problem to solve.

1. **Sewage:** In developing countries most of the waste water is discharged directly into streams, rivers and oceans without treatment, thus polluting the water and causing diseases. Leaking septic tanks and other sources of sewage can cause groundwater and stream contamination.

2. **Nutrients and chemical fertilizers:** Farmers add nutrients to the soil and the excess drains into rivers and seas. Together, sewage and fertilizers can cause a massive increase in the growth of algae or plankton that overwhelms huge areas of

oceans, lakes, or rivers. The algae is harmful because it removes oxygen from the water thus killing other forms of life, leading to what is known as a dead zone.

Polluted river water

3. **Industrial waste:** Industries produce huge amount of waste which contains toxic chemicals and pollutants such as lead, mercury, sulphur, asbestos, nitrates and many other harmful chemicals. Lack of proper waste management system results in industries draining the waste in the fresh water which goes into rivers, canals and later into the sea. The toxic chemicals have the capability to change the colour of water, increase the amount of minerals, change the temperature of water and therefore pose a serious hazard to water organisms.
4. **Mining activities:** Mining is the process of crushing the rock and extracting minerals from underground. These elements when extracted in the raw form, contain harmful chemicals and can increase the amount of toxic elements which may result in health problems. Mining activities emit several metal wastes from the rocks and are harmful for the environment.
5. **Marine dumping:** Garbage in the form of paper, aluminium, rubber, glass, plastic and food is collected and deposited into the sea in many cities. These items take many years to decompose.

Effect of oil spill

When such items enter the sea, they not only cause water pollution but also harm animals in the sea.

6. **Accidental oil leakage:** Oil spill pose a huge concern as large amount of oil enters into the sea and does not dissolve with water; thereby causing problem to local marine life such as fish, birds and marine animals.
7. **Burning of fossil fuels:** Fossil fuels like coal and oil, when burnt produce substantial amount of ash in the atmosphere. The particles which contain toxic chemicals when mixed with water vapour result in acid rain.
8. **Chemical fertilizers and pesticides:** Chemical fertilizers and pesticides are used by farmers to protect crops from insects and bacteria. They are also useful for plants growth. However, when it rains, the chemicals mix with rainwater and flow down into rivers and canals which pose serious damage for aquatic animals.

Minimizing Water Pollution and Improving the Environment

To keep the water clean and uncontaminated a number of factors must be kept in mind.

1. Eco-friendly chemicals should be used to replace toxic cleaning chemicals, sprays and other supplies. Even eco-friendly chemicals should be disposed of properly and with caution.
2. Factories and chemical plants that create large amounts of pollution should make sure that their waste is being disposed of properly. Proper disposal/containment of toxic chemicals

and materials, before they have an opportunity to reach the water bodies, would go a long way towards improving the current condition of water.

3. Toxic fumes created from industrial zones should be filtered, rerouted and cleaned before making their way to the atmosphere. Toxic fumes can cause acid rain.
4. By implementing renewable energy sources to run operations, companies can obtain their energy from eco-friendly sources that do not harm or pollute the atmosphere and thereby not pollute the water as well.
5. Reduce, recycle & reuse. Companies can find better ways to reduce the amount of materials they use to create their products, recycle left over materials and reuse or re-purpose materials that may not work with their existing products.

These are just some of the steps that can be taken to reduce toxic waste and pollutants that reach the water.

LAND POLLUTION

Land pollution, means degradation or destruction of earth's surface and soil, directly or indirectly as a result of human activities. Man carries out activities citing development, and the same affects the land negatively resulting in land pollution. The degradation of land that could be used constructively, in other words, is land pollution.

Causes of Land Pollution

1. **Degenerative actions:** The severity of human actions, like deforestation, overuse of pesticides and chemical fertilizers,

desertification, mining, inefficient or inadequate waste treatment, landfill etc. have resulted in degradation of land.

2. **Misuse of land:** This mainly refers to cutting trees to clear land for agriculture, or overusing the land beyond the carrying capacity of land resulting in desertification.
3. **Soil Pollution:** It is when the top-most soil layer of land is destroyed or polluted. Soil pollution affects not only the land, but also a lot of other things such as forest cover of a region and productivity of land in terms of agriculture, grazing etc. Soil pollution is also caused due to wrong agricultural practices, such as overuse of chemical fertilizers and pesticides.
4. **Radioactive waste:** Nuclear energy is produced using nuclear fission or fusion. The element that is used in production of nuclear energy is Uranium which is a highly toxic chemical. The nuclear waste that is produced by radioactive material needs to be disposed off to prevent any nuclear accident. Nuclear waste can have serious environmental hazards if not disposed of properly. Accidents have already taken place in Russia and Japan.
5. Other key causes of land pollution include urbanization, improper waste disposal, industrial activities, nuclear research, chemicals released by various heavy industries, coal- fired power plants, metals production industries, etc.

Effects of Land Pollution

1. **Effect on climate:** Land pollution results in loss of forest cover on earth. This in turn, affects the amount of rain which means

lesser vegetation. The effect of all different kinds of pollutions eventually leads to problems like acid rains, greenhouse effect and global warming.

2. **Extinction of species:** Species are pushed towards becoming endangered and extinct primarily by habitat fragmentation and urban sprawl. Land pollution destroys the natural habitat of animals. Both the actions can cause some species to go extinct and others to become invasive.
3. **Bio-magnification:** In this process, certain nondegradable substances go on accumulating in the food-chain. The most common example is of methyl mercury in fish and mercury in eagles. Not only does the bio-magnification put the particular species at risk, it puts all the species above and below it at risk, and ultimately affects the food pyramid.
4. **Effect on biodiversity:** Species extinction and bio-magnification is going to overthrow the balance of nature very significantly. The main reason for this is the disturbance created in the food chain example- on account of bio-magnification of mercury in eagles; they might go extinct in the subsequent years. However, we know eagles prey on snakes. Less (or no) eagles will then result in more number of snakes.

Prevention of Land Pollution

1. **Personal level:** We can make the following choices at a personal level– Encourage organic farming, buy organic food, dispose garbage by segregating it, say no to plastic, encourage

recycling, restrict the use of herbicides and pesticides in our own backyard as well.

2. **Disposal of waste:** Proper waste management is most important for the prevention of land pollution. Several steps should be taken to ensure that the waste gets disposed in the most harmless way, i.e. produce less or no toxins.

3. **Recycling and reuse:** Buy and use products that have been recycled. Use jute and cloth bags. Reusing old items is another good way to reduce the stress on various resources. Clothes, paper, glass, everything should be recycled and reused, as far as possible.

4. **Biodegradable products:** People should buy biodegradable products. 'Go Organic' is the mantra for avoiding land pollution.

5. **Grow more trees:** Initiative should be taken to grow more trees. Researches show that trees can actually fertilize the soil.

6. **Initiative both by individuals and authorities:** Awareness should be spread amongst the common people, to use organic, biodegradable products and to use resources efficiently. The industries too should follow proper procedures of industrial waste disposal. The government should strictly enforce laws for protection of the environment.

NOISE POLLUTION

By definition, the term noise pollution is usually applicable to sounds or noises that are unnatural in either their volume or their production. Noise pollution takes place when there is either excessive amount of noise or an unpleasant sound that causes temporary disruption in the natural balance.

Causes of Noise Pollution

1. **Poor urban planning:** In most of the developing countries, poor urban planning, congested houses, large families sharing small space, fight over parking, frequent fights over basic amenities leads to noise pollution which may disrupt the environment of the society.

2. **Industrialization:** Industrial noise comes from manufacturing plants such as fans, motors, and compressors mounted on the outside of buildings. Noise in the manufacturing unit can also be transmitted to the community through open windows and doors, and even through building walls. These noise sources have significant impacts on industrial workers, among whom noise-induced hearing loss is unfortunately common.

3. **Social events:** Noise is at its peak in most of the social events. People play songs on full volume which disturbs the neighbourhood. In the markets, call outs to attract the customer disturb the people.

4. **Transportation:** Large number of vehicles on roads, air planes flying over houses and underground trains produce loud noise. Increasing traffic gives rise to traffic jams in congested areas. Repeated use of the horn by impatient drivers adds to the increase in noise level.

5. **Construction activities:** Construction of bridges, buildings, stations, roads, flyovers take place in almost every part of the world. These construction activities and equipments are noisy.
6. **Household chores:** We are surrounded by gadgets and use them extensively in our daily life.

   Gadgets like TV, mobile, mixer grinder, pressure cooker, vacuum cleaners, washing machine and dryer, cooler and air conditioners are also minor contributors to the amount of noise that is produced.

While this form of pollution may seem harmless, it in fact has far reaching consequences and adverse effects on the health of the environment.

Effects of Noise Pollution

1. **Health issues:** Excessive noise pollution can influence psychological health. Studies show that the occurrence of aggressive behaviour, disturbance of sleep, constant stress, fatigue and hypertension can be linked to excessive noise levels.
2. **Hearing problems:** Constant exposure to loud levels of noise can result in the damage of our ear drums and loss of hearing. It also reduces our sensitivity to sounds that our ears pick up unconsciously to regulate our body's rhythm.
3. **Sleeping disorders:** Loud noise can certainly hamper sleeping pattern and may lead to irritation and fatigue.
4. **Cardiovascular issues:** Blood pressure levels, cardiovascular disease and stress related heart problems are on the rise. Studies

show that high intensity noise causes high blood pressure and increases heart beat rate as it disrupts the normal blood flow.

5. **Trouble communicating:** High decibel noise does not allow people to communicate freely. Constant sharp noise can result in severe headache and disturb one's emotional balance.
6. **Effect on wildlife:** Wildlife faces far more problems than humans because of noise pollution since they are more dependent on sound to track they prey, their mates and the young ones. Animals develop a better sense of hearing than us since their survival depends on it.

Solutions to Control Noise Pollution

Tree Plantation: Effective solution for noise pollution is to plant bushes and trees around the sound generating sources. Sound passage is blocked by the dense shrubs and trees. Trees can be planted in the surrounding area to live peacefully.

Soundproof homes: To block unwanted noise from outside, soundproof doors and windows can be installed.

Loudspeaker prohibition: The major cause of noise pollution in public areas is loudspeaker.

Strict laws should be imposed against those who violate and use loudspeakers in crowded areas and public places.

Factory location: Factories and industries should be located away from residential areas.

Machine quality: The quality of machines should be optimized to reduce sound production.

Lubrication of the machinery and servicing should be done to minimize noise generation.

Other solutions: Noise pollution at home is caused by using music systems and television sets with high volumes. Instead of using these appliances with the high volume, it is better to keep it at a moderate level. To wear ear protection while working in noisy conditions is an effective way to manage noise.

White Noise Machine:

For overcoming the effects of noise pollution the latest technology is using white noise machine. This device converts the unbearable noise into pleasant sound. A white noise machine is placed between the source of noise and the receptor. It produces soft sound like that of a waterfall fan and soft music.

Our Clean Future

Life is ultimately about choices—and so is pollution. We can live with sewage-strewn beaches, polluted rivers, and fish that are poisonous to eat or we can work together to keep the environment clean so the plants, animals, and people who depend on it remain healthy. We can take action at an individual level, community level as countries and continents to pass laws that will make the world less polluted. Working together, we can make pollution less of a problem— and the world a better place.

Depletion of Natural Resources and Ecological Imbalance

All the material and energy essential for survival and welfare of living beings including humans are provided by nature. They are called **natural resources**. The sustenance and welfare of mankind depend upon the exploitation of different natural resources.

ACTIVITY

Reflection

Aim: Learning to be solution oriented

Procedure: From the pictures given below of products and facilities we use in our daily life choose any one and explain briefly how it degrades the environment and what according to you is a solution which will be acceptable to all.

Ecology is the study of the relationships between living organisms, including humans, and their physical environment; All living and non-living things on earth are interrelated and thus are interdependent. If these balances and interdependences are sufficiently altered it upsets nature's equilibrium and results in ecological disturbances and environmental degradation. These resources have no doubt changed the level of living standard of man but at the same time have also disturbed the ecological balance.

With the development of modern industry and technology, the issue of ecological imbalance is of utmost importance. Much of what has been destroyed; unfortunately we will not be able to recover. Ecological imbalance between the natural factors and human activities results in socio-ecological crisis. This means that the balance between the environment and society is broken. The reasons for ecological imbalances are associated with the increasing industrialization, deforestation, water pollution and irrational waste of natural resources. In order to live in a wholesome environment there is dire need to identify the causes for degradation of the environment and to suggest responses and alternate causes of action.

FACTORS NECESSARY TO RESTORE ECOLOGICAL BALANCE CONSERVATION OF FOREST

Forest conservation is the practice of planning and maintaining forested areas for the benefit and sustainability of future generations. It involves the upkeep of the natural resources within a forest that are beneficial to both humans and the ecosystem. Forests provide suitable habitat for wild life along with filtering of groundwater and preventing runoff. Trees are mankind's lifeline. Not only do the trees act as purifiers of air, and receptacles of our waste products, trees have economic value too, we get fuel, fodder, timber, medicines and numerous other valuable products.

Conservation of forest in India

Today felling of trees and diverting land for other purposes have all taken its toll on forests. For sustaining ecological balance it is important that at least one third of the land is covered with forests. However, today in India we have less than 20% area under forests and much of it is degraded. Thus the need of the hour is to work towards saving existing forests and help in bringing larger areas under forests.

The Ministry of Environment and Forests (MoEF) is the nodal agency in the administrative structure of the Central Government for planning, promotion, co-ordination and overseeing the implementation of India's environmental and forestry policies and programmes. **Forest Survey of India (FSI)** is an organization under the Ministry of Environment & Forests, Government of India its principal mandate is to conduct survey and assessment of forest resources in the country. **The Forest Research Institute** promotes research in forestry and allied sciences and the Indian Institute of Forest Management looks after the forest management

To stop the degradation of forest there was a need to involve the public and so initiatives like social forestry scheme, one tree for every child, trees for eco-development have been taken up by the government. An innovative scheme to involve industries and private parties in afforestation drives was launched under industrial plantation. An attempt was made to make use of the waste lands, marginal lands and desert lands, energy plantations, fodder plantations etc. However forests are still being cut and degraded and wildlife still destroyed.

Presently, forests are being used for mainly two purposes, fuel wood and timber, both of which involve the felling of trees. This can be avoided by developing alternative sources of energy like solar, bio-gas etc. or by growing at least one tree for each tree cut. Secondly, new and better means of using forests should be evolved. For example– sericulture, bee keeping, etc. are not only viable but also very profitable alternatives. At the same time, forests should be protected as a system. This means that mono cultures are avoided and variety of trees suitable to the local environs is grown.

Figures extrapolated from the 2015 Forest Survey of India's biennial report show that while 2,511 sq km of prime forests have disappeared altogether, 1,135 sq km of non-forest areas have become either very dense or mid-dense forests during that time. But this can hardly offset the loss, because these new forests are mostly plantations or areas that were already forests, but had not been recorded until now. Even accounting for the non-forest areas now recorded as dense and mid-dense forests, the net loss of forests in these prime categories works out to be 1,376 sq km — more than twice the area of Mumbai — in two years.

Conserving and Utilizing Water Resources Scientifically

Being one of the wettest countries India still suffers from flood and droughts due to faulty utilization of water resources. After independence emphasis was laid on the development of big dams. River valley projects and big dams have multipurpose uses and have been known as the temples of modern India– for example Bakhra Nangal on the Sutlej river and Tehri dam on river Bagirathi. However, construction of big dams caused several ecological problems. There was large scale destruction of forest which altered the natural ecological balance of the region. Floods, droughts and landslides become prevalent in such areas. Tribal people, their life and culture which is deeply interrelated with the forest were uprooted causing socio-economic problem of displacing the tribal and native people of the region.

Today with growing demand of water for agriculture, industries and increasing urbanization there is a need to address the challenges of water scarcity. The government has taken several steps to address the challenges. Civic bodies like the Panchayat and Municipality have a water conservation strategy suited to the region example ground water recharge, rain water harvesting, renovation and maintenance of water bodies. For irrigation, the implementation of policies for the use of water must be efficient, economic, and rational. Water conservation and management can be better served through appropriate incentive and penalties.

Scientific Mining Practices

Mining an important economic activity results in ecological disturbances. Extraction of metal from under the ground results in pits and tunnels, toxic gases, incidents of fire pollution of underground water and collapse of the roof of caves causing accidents like the Chasnala tragedy. Opencast mining leads to defacing and destroying the landscape example in Uttrakhand mining has resulted in land slide, soil erosion and declining forest area. The disposal of mining waste, mineral dust from mines is constantly polluting the air and land and thus also reducing agricultural productivity. Mining also at times lead to change in soil chemistry and sometimes toxic material may enter the food chain through the process of bio-magnifications. Mining operations are also responsible for various health hazards to human beings in the form of respiratory problem and other illness.

Coal extraction

- **Scientific mining and conservation of minerals:** Advanced scientific mining technologies ensure conservation of minerals. Innovative ore extraction techniques are used to ensure minimum waste.
- **Protection of water resources at mines:** Mining operations should ensure that there is no intersection of the ground water table thus stopping the water from contamination.

- **Minimizing biodiversity impacts:** No national parks, wild life sanctuaries, corridors and tiger reserves should exist close to the mining area.
- Restoration of mined out land should be an important objective.

Mining should be done in a scientific manner. It can become more environmentally sustainable by developing and integrating practices that reduce the environmental impact of mining operations. These practices include measures such as reducing water and energy consumption, minimizing land disturbance and waste production, preventing soil, water, and air pollution at mine sites, and conducting successful mine closure and reclamation activities. When active mining ceases, mine facilities and site should be reclaimed and closed. Every proposed mining project must include a detailed discussion of the mine reclamation and closure. The plans must describe in detail how the mining company will restore the site to a condition that most resembles pre-mining environmental quality and also explain how it will prevent the release of toxic contaminants from various mine facilities such as abandoned open pits and keep aside funds to insure the costs of reclamation and closure. The objective should always be to return the site to a condition that most resembles the pre-mining condition.

Protect the Environment from Industrial and Atmospheric Pollution: In India, unplanned and uncontrolled growth of industries and ill-maintained automobiles are creating huge atmospheric pollution regularly. The main atmospheric pollutants include carbon dioxide, carbon monoxide, oxides of nitrogen, sulphur dioxide, hydrocarbon and metallic traces. Industrial wastes coming out of fertilizer factories, paper mills, leather factories without being treated are discharged in rivers, lakes and seas, creating huge health hazards for the population of the country.

To protect the environment we need to

- Spread social awareness about the dangers of pollution and make it a mass movement.
- Check population growth.
- Strict application of environment conservation acts and laws.
- Control over industrial and agricultural pollution.
- Extensive afforestation campaign should be launched in the interest of environment protection.
- River waters should be made clean.
- Provision should be made to supply clean drinking water to the rural population.
- Planned management of solid waste.

To conclude, it is said that economic development and environment protection should be made complementary to each other. Clean environment is the basic requirement of healthy living.

Wildlife Conservation in India

Ecologically, India can be divided into three main regions: the Himalayan Mountain system; the peninsular India sub region (woodlands and desert); and the tropical rain forest region. A great wealth of biological diversity exists in these regions and in India's wetlands and marine areas. Years of mismanagement, however, have degraded our forests, coastline, and poisoned our aquifers. Today,

India contains 172 species (2.9% of the world's total number) of animals that are considered to be globally threatened by the IUCN. Some of them are black buck, chinkara, wolf, swamp deer, nilgai, Indian gazelle, antelope, tiger, rhinoceros, Gir lion, crocodile, flamingo, pelican, bustard, white crane, grey heron, mountain quail.

Most recent extinctions can be attributed, either directly or indirectly, to human demographic and technological expansion, commercialized exploitation of species, and human-caused environmental change. These factors, in turn, have affected the reproductive rate of endangered species and their adaptability to changing environmental conditions.

ACTIVITY

Game Of Recall

Aim: Identification and Comprehension

Procedure: Identify the names of the endangered animals and bird shown below.

In Indian government and NGOs are taking keen interest in protection of wildlife. The Wild Life Protection Act, 1972, has several provisions for the conservation of wildlife. Wildlife Sanctuaries and National Parks, for example– Corbett National Park, Kanha National Park and Sariska Wildlife Sanctuary have been developed to protect the natural habitat of the wild animals. To prevent the poachers from entering the parks, the concerned park authorities have taken several actions which include fencing the park, regular patrolling and setting up anti- poaching team undertaken by the forest officials.

Some measures to protect the wildlife are by launching projects to keep the animals safe from the poachers and increase their count by way of breeding .

Project Tiger

Several tiger conservation efforts have been made to contain their shrinking numbers and the most popular one is the "Project Tiger" rolled out in the year 1973.

Project Elephant

Launched in February 1992 by the Government of India, Project Elephant has been designed to combine the programs for the conservation of elephant and its natural habitat. The other measures to protect the wildlife are; protecting the habitat of the animal by protecting the forests; protecting the wildlife from pollution and natural hazards, imposing restrictions on export and import of wildlife products and severe punishment for those who indulge in this activity; making special arrangements to protect those species whose number are limited; developing general awareness at national and international level regarding protection of wildlife.

Global Concern for the Protection of the Environment

Man has improved the technologies and other means necessary for production of wealth and exploited nature for his benefits without any forethought to the implications of his actions. Increasing industrialization has resulted in urban migration, slum development, deforestation, desertification resulting in degradation of the environment which we all share globally.

ACTIVITY

Share 1 Get 1

Aim:

- Comprehension and summarization of the study material

Procedure:

- After the concepts are shared, ask the students to process what they have learnt by asking them to draw a grid of nine squares. The grids need to be big enough to cover half a page in the notebook. In any of the three squares they can write any three factors necessary to restore ecological balance and write one point under each sub point. They can then work in teams and ask other students to fill the remaining unfilled portions of the grid. Each student can add only one idea to a student's grid. The task is complete when six students have filled up the remaining squares.
- Time taken should be approximately ten minutes.

After the grid is complete with all nines squares filled, the student will write a summary of all the points collected.

Share 1 Get 1

Wildlife Conservation in India	Project Tiger & Project Elephant		
Scientific Mining Practice	Bio magnification		
Conservation of forest	Social Forestry Scheme		

In the late 60s and 70s man's impact on the environment could be seen and felt. Rampant erosion, pollution, environmental degradation was occurring and was being experienced by man. It was only then that the responsibility to protect the health and well-being of the ecosystem began to dawn on the collective consciousness of the nations across the world. The leaders and environmentalist all expressed universal concern about the healthy and sustainable use of the planet. The initial concept of sustainable development was introduced in 1972 and was globally accepted as a vision recognizing the inter-connectedness of social, economic, and environmental issues. Certainly, no one nation can achieve sustainable development alone. Governments, businesses, and civil society have accepted this model as essential for making progress on the three pillars of sustainable development—social, economic, and environmental.

'The pursuit of sustainable development is a balancing act: it requires the implementation of policies, strategies, programs, and projects that treat environment and development as a single issue; it also demands changes in the mind sets, attitudes and behaviours of stakeholders'.

Asian Development Bank

The time line lists the major landmark in implementing policies, strategies, programs and projects for a sustainable environment.

1972- The United Nations Conference on the Human Environment was held in Stockholm. It lead to the establishment of numerous national environmental protection agencies and the United Nations Environment Programme (UNEP).

1973- The Chipko Movement in India was started in response to deforestation and environmental degradation, influencing forestry practices and women's participation in environmental issues.

1983- Secretary-General of the United Nations invited Dr. Gro Harlem Brundtland, former Prime Minister of Norway, to establish and chair a World Commission on Environment and Development.

1987- The World Commission on Environment and Development published "Our Common Future," also known as the Brundtland Report; it wove together social, economic, cultural, and environmental issues and global solutions; it popularized the term "sustainable development." The Montreal Protocol on Substances that Deplete the Ozone Layer was adopted. The world's population reached 6 billion.

2000- The United Nations Millennium Summit agreed to a set of time-bound and measurable goals for combating poverty, hunger, disease, illiteracy, environmental degradation, and discrimination against women; the Millennium Development Goals were to be achieved by 2015.

2005- The Kyoto Protocol entered into force legally binding developed country parties to goals for greenhouse gas emission reductions and establishing the Clean Development Mechanism for developing countries.

2007- The Inter governmental Panel on Climate Change published its fourth assessment report on climate change; the report stated that climate change policies were best addressed by integrating them within the broader framework of sustainable development strategies.

Former United States Vice-President Al Gore's documentary, "An Inconvenient Truth," won an Academy Award; the alarming forecasts of the Intergovernmental Panel on Climate Change about the planet's health made headlines; the Intergovernmental Panel on Climate Change and Al Gore shared the Nobel Peace Prize.

2011– The world's population reached seven billion.

2012– The United Nations Conference on Sustainable Development was held in Rio de Janeiro to mark the 20th anniversary of the 1992 United Nations Conference on Environment and Development and the 10th anniversary of the 2002 World Summit on Sustainable Development in Johannesburg; it focused on two themes: a green economy in the context of sustainable development, poverty eradication, and the institutional framework for sustainable development.

World leaders at Rio +20

2016 – The 17 Sustainable Development Goals (SDGs) of the 2030 Agenda for Sustainable Development were adopted by world leaders in September 2015 at an historic UN Summit at the at the United Nations Headquarters in New York — officially came into force. Over the next fifteen years, with these new Goals that universally apply to all, countries will mobilize efforts to end all forms of poverty, fight inequalities and tackle climate change, while ensuring that no one is left behind.

ACTIVITY

Project: Count your carbon foot prints

Aim: Critical thinking skills - learning to evaluate

Procedure:

- Students can be asked to measure their carbon foot prints in a period of 24 hours. They will find solutions to reduce the carbon footprints in school and also at home.
- Intra class competition can be held to see what measures each section has taken to reduce the carbon foot prints. The site mentioned below will help the students understand how to measure carbon foot prints.

4 The State and the Nation

What is a nation? What is a state? Are they the same? Yes of course.... Oh... well I think so.... maybe not...

Our view about the nation and the state are often confusing. Many a times they have been used interchangeably for each other. For a common man there seems to be little difference between the two, but as students of General Studies we must try and understand the difference between them and what stems out when they are put together.

- For an entity to be considered a state, four fundamental conditions must be met
  - A state must have a territorial base.
  - A stable population must reside within its borders.
  - There should be a government to which this population owes allegiance.
  - A state has to be recognized diplomatically by other states.
- A nation is a group of people who share a set of characteristics. At the core of the concept of a nation is the notion that people having commonalities, owe their allegiance to the nation and to its legal representative - the state. The recognition of commonalities among people spread with new technologies

and education. With improved methods of transportation and invention of the printing press, people could travel, witnessing firsthand similarities and differences among people.

NATION STATE

The **nation state** is a system of organization in which people with a common identity live inside a country with firm borders and a single government. The nation state has a huge influence on the way we live our lives. It's how we identify ourselves. I'm American. I'm Russian. I'm Indian. It also determines what language we speak, what laws we follow, and what holidays we celebrate. The nation state is a system of political, geographical and cultural organization, and it is one of the most important parts of our life. The nation state is held together by its physical boundaries, its government and the fact that the people believe they are connected to each other.

This coincidence between state and nation, the nation-state, is the foundation for national self-determination, the idea that peoples sharing nationhood have a right to determine how and under what conditions they should live.

Other nations are spread among several states; in these cases, the state and the nation do not coincide.

- It may be a state with several nations, like South Africa and India.
- In the case of the United States and Canada, the state and nation do not coincide, yet a common identity and nationality is forged over time, even in the absence of religious, ethnic, or cultural similarity.

- In the United States, national values reflecting commonly held ideas are expressed in public rituals.

Disputes over state territories and the desires of nations to form their own states have been major sources of instability and even conflict. History has many examples to explain the same–

- The conflict between the Israeli Jews and Palestinian Arabs, who each claim the same territory.
- India which is one of the best examples of a nation -
  - A state which has well defined natural boundaries that are an effective defence against aggressive invaders.
  - A common history that binds us together, and the most important.
  - Diverse culture that has been a source of unity above everything else.

Group Discussion

Divide the class in two groups'. Each belonging to one community-Jews and Palestine. Each group should put forward their point of view about the situation.

CULTURE

Indian culture has always been enriched by external and internal influences. We have borrowed, accommodated and assimilated heavily from different groups and made it our own. For example, our music today embodies influence from all over the world.

To quote Pt. Nehru "Some kind of unity has occupied the mind of India since the dawn of civilization. That unity was not conceived of as something imposed from outside. It was something deeper and within its fold, the widest tolerance of belief and custom was practiced and every variety acknowledged and even encouraged."

Cultural appropriation is the adoption or use of one culture by members of another culture.

Having understood that one should also have a clear view how through a passage of time the same idea of cultural unity has been threatened by various incidents in both pre and post independent India.

ACTIVITY

Make a note of your daily activities and write down the products used through the day. The concept of cultural appropriation has seeped into our lives without us even realizing it.

The magnitude of violence that was perpetuated during the colonial times; the policy of divide and rule or with the partition of India; Post 1947 — the Sikh riots of 1984 and the Gujrat riots of 2002 have tested the very foundation of our existence as a country which believes that diversity is our biggest strength.

Our constitution makers were well aware that our diversity can be challenged at different times and by different groups of people and hence made adequate provisions in the constitution to safeguard the rights of the people of India. The Fundamental Rights given in Part III of the constitution not only uphold but also encourage our diversity.

Right to Freedom of Religion (Art.25-26)

Cultural and Educational Rights of minority groups (Art.29 -30)

RELIGION

Religion to some is the practicing of some beliefs and rituals. To another person it is the presence of some supernatural powers. For some it's like an ever growing organism which is paramount in a person's everyday life.

There is no one definition of religion which can be said to be absolute and followed in the world.

The world has varied religions that are followed by the people. In fact all religions have something specific to teach its disciples which may be distinct. But certain postulates are universal and overlapping.

Our religious thought process has been shaped by studying the views of **Ashoka, Akbar**, the **Bhakti movement**, **Sufism**, etc. Further, they have been re-affirmed by modern western influences which has helped in the progressive growth of both all communities.

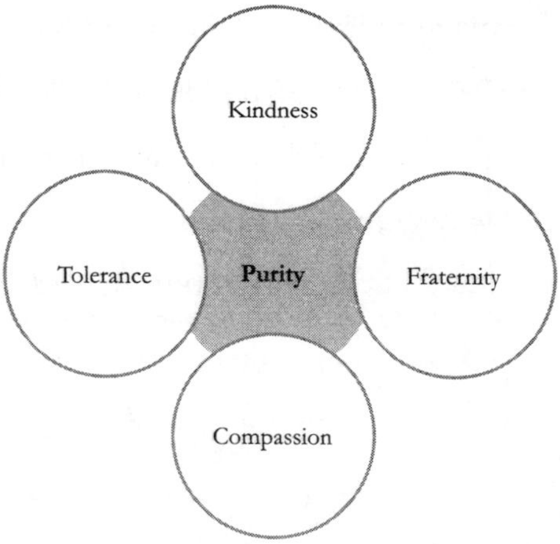

INDIA'S LANGUAGE DIVERSITY

The source of most of the Indian languages has been the Vedas.

	**Vedas** The holy book of Hindu religion, they are believed to be one of the oldest books written by mankind. The four vedas are - Rigveda, Yajurveda, Samaveda and Atharvaveda

Panini a well-known grammarian polished the Vedas and the revised language was Sanskrit which further is known as the mother of many languages. The similarity which runs through the northern languages or the use of certain Sanskrit words in southern languages prove a close affinity among Indian languages. Sanskrit retains a pan-India character.

* **Ashoka -** Ruler of Mauryan dynasty from 268 to 232 BCE
* **Akbar -** 1556 to 1605 BCE; Started his own religion Din-i-ilahi
* **Bhakti movement -** 7th to 12th century
* **Sufism -** 12th to 18th Century

India is a land of diversity. We have 18 major languages and as many as 844 dialects.

Most Widely Spoken Indian Languages by Number of Native Speakers

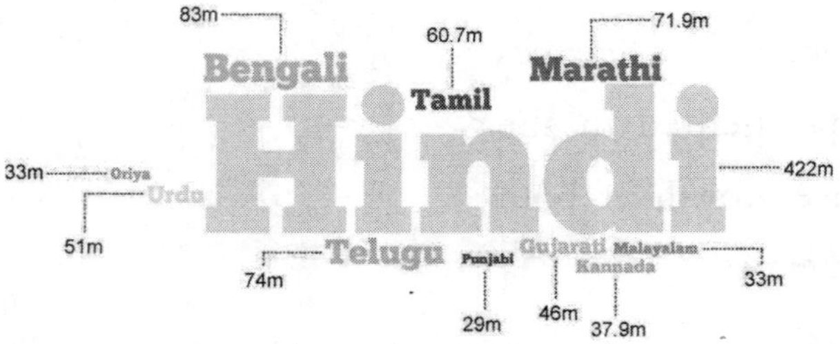

As seen above Hindi is the most spoken language in the country. Hindi also happens to be the co-officiating language for all official work of the government. The Constitution of India designates the official language of the Government of India as Hindi in the Devanagari script, as well as English.

DEBATE ABOUT ADOPTION OF HINDI AS OFFICIAL LANGUAGE OF INDIA

It was as early as 1918, that Mahatma Gandhi propagated Hindustani (Hindi + Urdu) as the lingua franca of our country. The issues had divided opinion among Annie Besant and Gandhiji.

This difference of opinion set the tone for this particular issue even post-independence. There was fierce debate in the House of Parliament about the language in which the Constitution would be written and the language in which the proceedings will be held. The House had divergent views of Hindi being adopted as the national language. Leaders from southern India firmly opposed the move.

National Language is the language spoken and written by majority of people in a country. It is also the official language of the country recognized and adopted by the country.	*Official Language is a language or languages that have special status in legal, political and educational life of a place.*

THE MUNSHI - AYYANGAR FORMULA (1949)

It was a compromise constitutional framing formula which shaped the official language policy of Republic of India. Part XVII of the constitution was drafted accordingly.

The First Official Language Commission (1956) and the Parliamentary Committee on Official language (1959) advocated Hindi to be used as primary language and English as secondary one. This led to major agitation among the non-Hindi speaking people. Nehru, the then Prime Minister of India included English in the Eight Schedule of the constitution to appease the situation.

Even with this, the anti-Hindi stance hardened over a period of time. To give legal backing to Nehru's assurance of 1959, the Official Language Act was passed in 1963. The three language formula recommended by the Madras C.M also increased student support for anti- Hindi cause.

The Madras State Anti-Hindi agitation was supported by the DMK which lasted for about 2 months in 1965. It led to deaths of several people and two people committed suicide by self-immolation on streets.

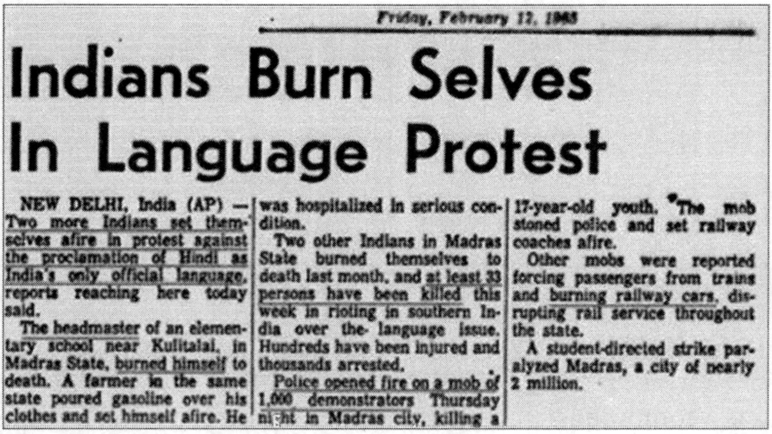

Friday, February 12, 1965

Indians Burn Selves In Language Protest

NEW DELHI, India (AP) — Two more Indians set themselves afire in protest against the proclamation of Hindi as India's only official language, reports reaching here today said.

The headmaster of an elementary school near Kulitalai, in Madras State, burned himself to death. A farmer in the same state poured gasoline over his clothes and set himself afire. He was hospitalized in serious condition.

Two other Indians in Madras State burned themselves to death last month, and at least 33 persons have been killed this week in rioting in southern India over the language issue. Hundreds have been injured and thousands arrested.

Police opened fire on a mob of 1,000 demonstrators Thursday night in Madras city, killing a 17-year-old youth. The mob stoned police and set railway coaches afire.

Other mobs were reported forcing passengers from trains and burning railway cars, disrupting rail service throughout the state.

A student-directed strike paralyzed Madras, a city of nearly 2 million.

To appease the situation, Shastrjii assured that-

- English would be used for Centre-State and intra-state communications.

◈ All India Civil Services Exam would be conducted in English.

◈ In February 1965, a resolution was passed by Congress working committee which stated that English would be the official language unless all states consent otherwise.

◈ The Official Language (amendment) Act, 1967, guaranteed the virtual indefinite policy of bilingualism in official transactions.

◈ The language issue over a period of time has lost its importance yet it continues to generate minor tension and often manifests itself as linguistic communalism in different states.

NATIONAL INTEGRATION

Diversity creates divide and also unites people. The National Integration Council was set up 1962 to address the problems of communalism, casteism and regionalism.

How can national integration be accomplished

◈ The first and the foremost step is to eradicate terrorism from the soil of India. Linguistic fanaticism should be suppressed.

◈ Fissiparous tendencies cannot be checked by force and the

compulsions of law. They have to be eradicated by persuasion and education.

- The battle of national integration is to be waged in the minds of men. All media of mass communications, such as social media, newspapers, radio and television must be utilized for a drive for promoting national unity.
- Educational system must be so reconstructed as to emphasize the composite nature of our culture and to instil in the minds of the youth a legitimate pride in our social heritage. Promotion of national integration should be made an integral part of our educational programme.
- There should be a positive change in the attitude of the majority community towards the minorities so that the latter join the main stream of the nation.
- Indian nationalism must fight the caste system tooth and nail. Students of minority communities should be offered equal opportunities for all jobs and services.
- Political parties have a significant role to play in shaping the national outlook. They need greater discipline and restraint in India than those in other countries. They must learn to subordinate other political ambitions, to the imperative need, of bringing various people together and they must train people to think in national terms.
- Finally, there can never be sense or unity of fellow feeling in a country where there are huge inequalities in the distribution of national income and wealth. The best way to achieve national

integration, to mobilize all our resources for rapid development and to achieve stability is to make the concept of Democratic Socialism a reality.

Democratic Socialism is a political ideology that advocates political democracy alongside social ownership of the means of production.

QUESTIONS

1. Define the term 'culture'. Why is the culture of India considered to be a synthesis of several cultures?
2. Why is it that India does not have a national language?
3. Write any two ways in which national integration can be achieved in India. Give examples to support your answer.

5 International Peace and Understanding

"Since wars are born in the minds of men, it is in the minds of men, that the defences of peace must be constructed."

Preamble to the UNESCO Constitution

PEACE

What is Peace?

One elementary way of defining peace has been to say that peace is absence of war. This is, however, a very narrow view of peace. No doubt, absence of war is the first condition of peace, yet peace is not merely an absence of war. It is in reality a condition characterised

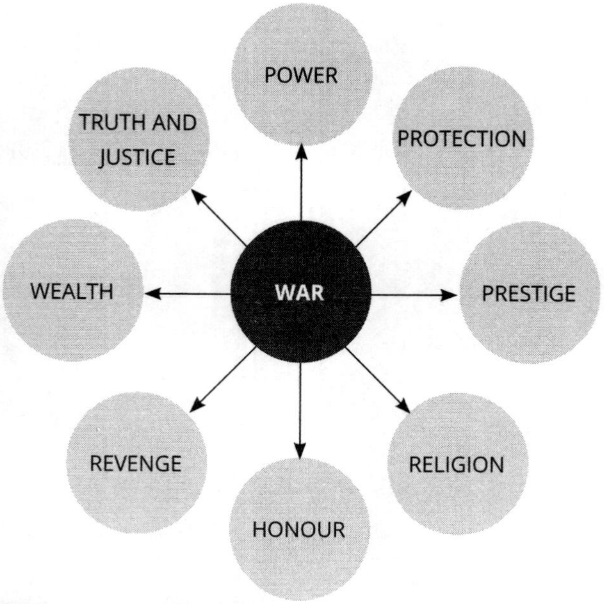

by peaceful, cooperative and harmonious conduct of international relations with a view to secure all-round sustainable development of the people of the world.

IMPORTANCE OF PEACE IN THE CONTEMPORARY ERA

The issue of war and peace has always been a focal issue in all periods of history and at all levels relations among nations. The concern of the humankind for peace can be assessed by taking into account the fact that all religions, all religious scriptures and several religious ceremonies are committed to the cause of peace and all these advocate an elimination of war. The Shanti Path recited by the Hindus, the sermons of Pope and the commands of all the holy scriptures of the Christians, Muslims, Hindus, Sikhs and all other communities hold out a sacred commitment to peace.

Horrors of War

Yet the international community fully realized the supreme importance of the virtue of peace against the evil of war only after having suffered the most unfortunate and highly destructive two World Wars in the first half of the 20th century. The blood-soaked shreds of humanity that lay scattered in several hundred battle grounds, particularly on the soils of Hiroshima and Nagasaki, cried for peace, peace and peace on the earth.

Moreover, in view of the development of nuclear armaments with the potential for mass destruction, man cannot afford to consider war as a necessary evil. It is a universally recognised fact that a global nuclear war would result in the destruction of not only the humankind but the entire planet. In this context, peace is not only important, it is very valuable today.

Here, it becomes pertinent to quote John Kennedy, the former President of USA, who had declared, "Mankind must put an end to war or war will put an end to mankind".

MEASURES TO ESTABLISH PEACE

Peace can be established without using violence. Let us discuss some measures that people of various nations have been using or trying to use to achieve peace between nations.

Removing the Source of Threat

Removing the source of threat to peace is a traditional concept. It is an effective way of avoiding an imminent conflict.

In such cases, the potential threat of aggression is thwarted by a sudden, swift and well planned action. The destruction of Iraqi nuclear reactor, engaged in manufacturing nuclear weapons, by an air attack by Israel, in 1981 is an excellent example in this regard.

Another example can be the declaration of war by the United States of America on Germany in 1917 which was called as 'a war to end war' by the then US President, Mr. Woodrow Wilson.

The Osirak reactor prior to the Israeli attack 1981

But once must keep in mind that 'removing the source of threat' measure should be universally recognised by the world society as morally justified.

Deterrence

This path of achieving peace is a better known and followed one: to avoid the circumstances/ situations which may lead to the disruption of peace.

Deterrence is a contingent threat: 'If you attack me, I will attack you', is the mantra here.

During the Cold War era (1945-1990), the principle of deterrence was in practise. The two super powers, namely, USA and USSR, were following this to avoid a confrontation.

Logic of 'deterrence' : Both the super powers have the capacity to retaliate against an attack from the other and cause a lot of destruction. Since the scale of destruction is so huge that neither can afford to initiate a war. Thus, the Cold War — despite being an intense form of rivalry between great powers – remained a 'cold' and not hot or shooting war.

The war that US and some of its allies fought against few years back could be possibly termed as USA's policy of deterrence. The policy of deterrence is also followed by a number of other countries whose regional, political or economic interests clash and which are traditionally hostile to each other.

Deterrence may succeed in averting war for some time but the peace it promises may break at any time. The success of deterrence depends on the belief held by the parties that there is no effective defence against the threat posed by their adversaries.

Non-Violent Non-Cooperation

There is another path to peace- the path of non-violence. Non-violence is an active and assertive approach in which the victim of aggression uses moral strength to thwart the wrong actions/ plans of the aggressor.

This measure is considered as the most respectable way to achieve peace as it is used only for defence.

So far, this approach has been tried in some countries to persuade unwilling rulers to agree to introduce desirable political decisions or change the policies. The best example is Gandhiji's non-violent Non-Cooperation movement to fight for India's freedom.

Another example of this is Martin Luther King's successful fight for rights and dignity of the Black community.

This approach certainly offers the prospect of significant political changes without war and violence. Non-violent action, is, therefore, is increasingly considered as one of the best "ways for attaining and preserving peace.

Disarmament

Disarmament is the act of reducing, limiting or abolishing weapons. Disarmament generally refers to a country's military or specific type of weaponry. Disarmament is often taken to mean total elimination of weapons of mass destruction, such as nuclear arms. General and Complete Disarmament was defined by the United Nations General Assembly as the elimination of all WMD, coupled with the "balanced reduction of armed forces and conventional armaments, based on the principle of undiminished security of the parties with a view to promoting or enhancing stability at a lower military level, considering the need of all States to protect their security."

NUCLEAR DISARMAMENT

Nuclear disarmament refers to both the act of reducing or eliminating nuclear weapons and to the end state of a nuclear-weapons-free world, in which nuclear weapons are completely eliminated.

Did You Know?

Only one country has been known to ever dismantle their nuclear arsenal completely—the apartheid government of South Africa apparently developed half a dozen crude fission weapons during the 1980s, but they were dismantled in the early 1990s.

World over, millions of people have demonstrated against nuclear weapons and for an end to the cold war arms race.

In recent years, many statesmen advocated nuclear disarmament and have called upon governments to embrace the vision of a world free of nuclear weapons.

Proponents of nuclear disarmament say that it would lessen the probability of nuclear war occurring, especially accidentally. Critics of nuclear disarmament say that it would undermine deterrence.

ARMS REDUCTION TREATIES

- Partial Test Ban Treaty (PTBT) 1963
- Nuclear Non-Proliferation Treaty (NPT) 1968
- Interim Agreement on Offensive Arms (SALT I) 1972
- Anti-Ballistic Missile Treaty (ABM) 1972
- Strategic Arms Limitation Treaty (SALT II) 1979
- Intermediate-Range Nuclear Forces Treaty (INF) 1987
- Strategic Arms Reduction Treat (START I)
- Strategic Arms Reduction Treat (START II) 1993
- Strategic Offensive Reductions Treaty (SORT) 2002
- Comprehensive Test Ban Treaty (CTBT) 1996
- New START Treaty 2010

Find out the provisions of NPT and the reasons behind the treaty being considered discriminatory.

INTERNATIONAL FORUMS OF COOPERATION: UNITED NATIONS*

The maintenance of international peace and security represents the primary purpose behind the establishment of the United Nations in 1945. It reflects the intentions and desires of its founders who sought to establish an international organization for achieving this

*Find out information on the formations of League of Nations and what led to its failure.

end. It is a prerequisite to any other purpose of the United Nations. Without it, no friendly relations, no international cooperation, and no harmonization of nation's actions could be achieved.

Because of the importance of international peace and security, the founders of the United Nations insisted on it and emphasized it in the Preamble and the Charter of the Organization. They stated all the possible principles, methods and procedures which are to be followed to attain this end.

The theme "we are going to create a collective security system, and this time we are going to make it work," dominated the entire process of planning and formulating the United Nations Charter. The Charter of the organisation provided a system for the pacific settlement or adjustment of disputes, and the use of collective measures in threat to or breaches of peace and acts of aggression.

The first method provided by the system is that of seeking peaceful settlement or adjusbnent of disputes and situation by peaceful means listed in the Charter. The second method is that of taking collective actions (measures) of a coercive nature for the prevention and removal of threats to the peace and for the suppression of acts of aggression and other breaches of the peace. Through these two methods delineated in Chapter VI entitled "Pacific Settlement of Disputes" and Chapter VII entitled "Actions with Respect to Threats to the Peace, Breaches of the Peace, and Acts of Aggression" of the Charter, the United Nations primarily exercises its role in maintaining international peace and security. This objective is achieved by the United Nations via its agencies:

United Nations Children's Fund

World Health Organization

United Nations Educational, Scientific and Cultural Organization

Food and Agriculture Organization

International Monetary Fund

International Labour Organization

International Development Association

International Court of Justice

The United Nations Children's Fund (UNICEF) is a United Nations (UN) programme headquartered in New York City that provides humanitarian and developmental assistance to children and mothers in developing countries. It is one of the members of the United Nations Development Group and its executive committee. UNICEF was created by the United Nations General Assembly on

11th December 1946, to provide emergency food and healthcare to children in countries that had been devastated by World War II. In 1953, UNICEF's mandate was extended to address the needs of children in the developing world and became a permanent part of the United Nations System. At that time, the words "international" and "emergency" were dropped from the organization's name, making it simply the United Nations Children's Fund, or popularly known as "UNICEF".

The World Health Organization (WHO) acts as a coordinating authority on international public health and deals with health and sanitation and diseases and sends medical teams to help combat epidemics. Established on 7th April 1948, and headquartered in Geneva, Switzerland, the agency inherited the mandate and resources of its predecessor, the Health Organization, which had been an agency of the League of Nations. It was established in April 7 (1948) when 26 members of the United Nations ratified its Constitution. April 7 is celebrated as the World Health Day every year. The WHO is governed by 194 Member States through the World Health Assembly. Its headquarters are at Geneva in Switzerland.

The United Nations Educational, Scientific and Cultural Organization (UNESCO) is a specialized agency of the United Nations established in 1946 with its headquarters in Paris, France. Its stated purpose is to contribute to peace and security by promoting international collaboration through education, science, and culture in order to further universal respect for justice, the rule of law, and the human rights and fundamental freedoms proclaimed in the UN Charter.

The Food and Agriculture Organization (FAO) of the United Nations leads international efforts to defeat hunger. Serving both developed and developing countries, FAO acts as a neutral forum where all nations meet as equals to negotiate agreements and debate policy. FAO's mandate is to raise levels of nutrition, improve agricultural productivity, better the lives of rural populations and contribute to the growth of the world economy. FAO is the largest of UN agencies and its headquarters is in Rome, Italy.

The International Labour Organization (ILO) deals with labour issues. Its headquarters are in Geneva, Switzerland. Founded in 1919, it was formed through the negotiations of the Treaty of Versailles, and was initially an agency of the League of Nations. It became a member of the UN system after the demise of the League and the formation of the UN at the end of World War II. Its Constitution, as amended to date, includes the Declaration of Philadelphia on the aims and purposes of the Organization. Its secretariat is known as the International Labour Office.

International Monetary Fund (IMF) is sometimes considered to be a specialized agency. It is part of the United Nations system and has a formal relationship agreement with the UN, but retains its independence. The IMF provides monetary cooperation and financial stability and acts as a forum for advice, negotiation and assistance on financial issues. It is headquartered in Washington, D.C., United States of America.

The International Development Association (IDA) is an international financial institution which offers concessional loans and grants to the world's poorest developing countries. The IDA is a member of the World Bank Group and is headquartered in Washington, D.C., United States. It was established in 1960 to complement the existing International Bank for Reconstruction and Development by lending to developing countries which suffer from the lowest gross national income, from troubled creditworthiness, or from the lowest per capita income. Together, the International Development Association and International Bank for Reconstruction and Development are collectively generally known as the World Bank, as they follow the same executive leadership and operate with the same staff.

The International Court of Justice, commonly referred to as the World Court or ICJ is the primary judicial branch of the United Nations (UN). Seated in the Peace Palace in The Hague, Netherlands, the court settles legal disputes submitted to it by states and provides advisory opinions on legal questions submitted to it by duly authorized international branches, agencies, and the UN General Assembly.

Other than the UNO, many regional organisations also work towards maintaining peace in their region:

REGIONAL ORGANISATIONS

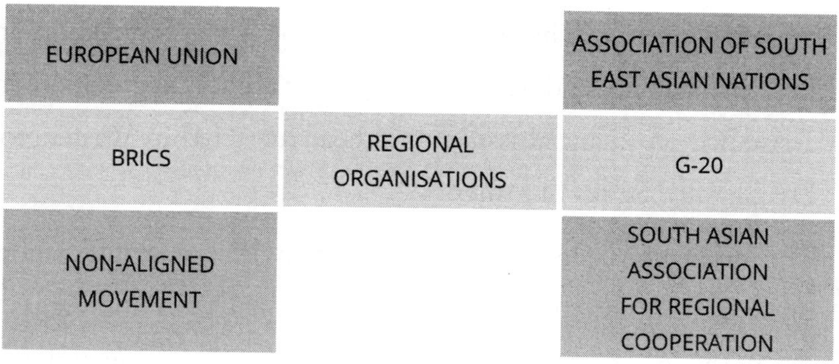

All of these organisations work towards minimizing conflicts and achieve peace as well as gain economic and political advantages through diplomacy.

QUESTIONS

1. "Mankind must put an end to war or war will put an end to mankind" Elaborate in four points.
2. Write down the organs of the United Nations Organisation.
3. Mention any two methods used by the UN to achieve its aim of international peace and security.
4. Suggest some ways to maintain peace in the world apart from the ones discussed in the chapter.
5. What are peace keeping operations? Write about any four such operations conducted by the UN.